DRUIDS

PREACHERS OF IMMORTALITY

ANNE ROSS

TEMPUS

For my husband
Richard W. Feachem

First published 1999
This edition published 2004

Tempus Publishing Limited
The Mill, Brimscombe Port,
Stroud, Gloucestershire, GL5 2QG
www.tempus-publishing.com

British Library Cataloguing in Publication Data.
A catalogue record for this book is available from the British Library.

ISBN 0 7524 2576 5

Typesetting and origination by Tempus Publishing Limited
Printed and bound in Great Britain

CONTENTS

ACKNOWLEDGEMENTS

I would like to record my debt of gratitude to my family and friends for all their encouragement down the years, which cannot be fully expressed in this brief statement. I would, however, wish to mention my deep indebtedness to my daughter, Berenice, for all her help in every way, and the numerous hours she has spent working with me in preparing the book for publication. Charles and Richard have both made their own, singular contributions, and to Richard I am especially indebted for his meticulous line drawings and maps. I would also like to record my gratitude to my publisher, Peter Kemmis Betty, for his kind consideration and patience.

Plate 2, The National Library of Wales; plate 3a, *Current Archaeology*; Plate 4a, BBC Chronicle; plate 7, J. Clarke; plate 8, The National Museum of Ireland; plate 17, Rupert Wace; plate 21, The British Museum; fig. 2, Stephen Mitchell; figs.4, 5, D. Srejovic; fig. 10, National Museum, Copenhagen; figs 11, 28, I.M. Stead; figs. 14, 51-3, Chris Rudd; fig. 17, R. Sheridan; fig. 25a, A. Chapman; fig. 55, Chris Rudd; figs 63, 64, J. Chivito; fig. 66, National Geographic Society.

PREFACE

The prehistory, protohistory and history of much of Europe west from the Urals and south from Prussia exhibits an unbroken series of material developments moving steadily onward from the establishment of the settled, rather than the nomadic, way of life. Evidence of this movement is seen in structures – dwellings and tombs – and in the progression from the use of stone through that of bronze to iron, in the manufacture of weaponry and other material objects.

While material changes took place steadily, the people remained much the same, judging by their skeletal remains.

Up to the 1960s material changes were generally accounted for by migration. Since then, however, this concept has been superseded by a realisation that there was no need for it; and the 'migration theory' is no longer heard except in uninformed echo.

In the first millennium BC the Greeks called those people *Keltoi* who used a certain language, the origin of which lay in the distant past. Those who lived in the region in which any version of this language was used were 'Celts', although they may well not have known it. Which people among the British before the seventeenth century, for example, would have called themselves *Europeans*? That word is first recorded in use in 1603 and, as meaning 'a native of Europe', in 1632.

Likewise, the peoples who lived alongside the Celts, but spoke their own languages, were not Celts. That is not to suggest, though, that they were any different in general behaviour or appearance from their Celtic neighbours.

In conversation with an Hungarian Museum Director from Budapest I happened to make reference to the Celts in central Europe. He instantly replied with great enthusiasm: 'In Hungary we are *all* Celts! Soldiers come, heroes fall – but *the people* go on!'

FOREWORD
The Celtic Languages

The Celtic languages – which belong to the so-called Indo-European group of related tongues – are very ancient, as is the entire Celtic tradition. They are divided by philologists into two main groups; the first of these is known as P-Celtic or Brythonic (Gaulish, Celt-Iberian, Lepontic (N. Italy) and British, now known as Welsh). This latter group includes Breton, spoken in Brittany, the terrain of the powerful Gaulish tribe the Veneti, who were subjugated by the Romans in 56 BC. In the sixth and seventh centuries AD incomers from south-west Britain, speaking Welsh, resettled the region and established the foundations of modern Brittany *(22)*. It is likely that native Veneti still remained and intermarried with the incomers.

The second group of Celtic origin is known as the Q-Celtic or Goidelic group, spoken by the Gaels. There is evidence that both P- and Q-Celtic were at one time used on the continent as place-names and deity names suggest. Moreover, the famous Coligny calendar employs both the P and Q forms. Ireland is named after its eponymous goddess Ériu and the genitive form of the name, Erin, came into common usage. Gaelic was also spoken in the Isle of Man and became the language of the North Western Highlands and Islands of Scotland from the fifth century AD.

The Picts of Scotland and probably Northern Ireland used a different language, possibly non-Indo-European in origin, although both Goidelic and Brythonic elements have been identified in their inscriptions and appear in their king-lists.

The Celtic languages changed and were modified with the passage of time and it can be confusing when we find that names are spelt in different ways according to the dates of the texts; for example, the divine hero can be spelt Fionn or Finn; the goddess Medb is spelt Maeve, and so on. It is a specialist subject and the reader is advised to consult such scholarly works as Professor Glanville Price's brilliantly edited *Encyclopedia of the Languages of Europe* (Blackwell, Oxford, 1998).

The problems of attempting to reconstruct an early society by way of linguistic evidence alone need not be emphasised and we are extremely fortunate to have the support of today's highly sophisticated archaeological techniques.

INTRODUCTION

They have philosophers and theologians who are held in
much honour and are called Druids; they have sooth-sayers
too of great renown who tell the future by watching the flights
of birds and by observation of the entrails of victims; and
everyone waits upon their word.

(Diodorus Siculus, *Histories*, V, 31, 2-5)

The early Celtic world:
its archaism, social structure and religious attitudes

The main sources for any study of Celtic origins and subsequent history are the inevitable travellers' tales which
contain some items of great interest; however, it must be noted
that they are of unequal quality and value. Nevertheless, they
provide us with some of our earliest glimpses into a rapidly
evolving Celtic world. Amongst these, of course, we must rate the
prolific, sometimes colourful, and perhaps not always exact
observations of the ethnographers. Used in conjunction with the
evidence for Celtic place and river names, some of which (especially the river names) must be of very great antiquity, they do
provide the framework at least, into which we may fit the pieces
of 'evidence' for the early Celtic world. Also there are the

comments of the Celtic world looking in upon itself – 'the Celts through Celtic eyes'. Finally, we depend for much information from the writings of the classics, first Greek and then Roman:

> Among all the Gallic peoples, generally speaking, there are three categories of men who are held in exceptional honour; the Bards, the Vates, and the Druids. The Bards are singers and poets; the Vates, diviners and natural philosophers; while the Druids, in addition to natural philosophy, study also moral philosophy. The Druids are considered the most just of men, and on this account they are entrusted with the decision, not only of the private disputes, but of the public disputes as well; so that, in former times, they even arbitrated cases of war, and made the opponents stop when they were about to line up for battle, and the murder cases in particular, had been turned over to them for decision. Further, when there is a big yield (of criminals for sacrifice) from these cases, there is forthcoming a big yield from the land, too, as they think. However, not only the Druids, but others as well, say that men's souls, and also the universe, are indestructible, although both fire and water will at some time or other prevail over them.
>
> (Strabo, *Geographica*, IV, 4, c. 197, 4)

> The common people are nearly regarded as slaves; they possess no initiative, and their views are never invited on any question. Most of them, being weighed down by debt or by heavy taxes, or by the injustice of the more powerful, hand themselves over into slavery to the upper classes, who all have the same legal rights against these men that a master has towards his slave. One of the two classes is that of the Druids, the other that of the knights. The Druids are concerned with the worship of the gods, look after public and private sacrifice, and expound religious matters. A large number of young men flock to them for training and hold them in high honour. For they have the right to decide nearly all public and private disputes and they also

pass judgment and decide rewards and penalties in criminal
and murder cases and in disputes concerning legacies and
boundaries.

(Caesar, *De Bello Gallico*, VI, 13, 1)

Next we proceed to documentary evidence in the vernacular
literature, particularly that of Ireland, supported or modified by
the Latin writings of the early Celtic church, which we may
regard as the 'pagans through Christian eyes' as most of the
priests of the Celtic church were Celts themselves. Fortunately
for our record, although claiming to abhor the more outra-
geously pagan practices of their − as yet − un-Christianised
fellow-countrymen, it is evident from the writings that they
were still under the spell of the heady poetry, with all its metrical complexity and close observation of the beauties and
wonders of nature which both pagan and Christian attributed to
God's creation or to that of the Druids who at some earlier stage
had claimed to having themselves created the world. Moreover,
their three fundamental precepts would have pertained equally
to pagan and Christian ethic. These were: 'Worship the gods; be
manly; tell the truth.'

This is of course a triadic concept, and as we shall see, the
number three and its products were of great sanctity and significance. Although the Druids did not commit their secret lore to
writing, for fear it might fall into hostile or irreverent hands,
they did use Greek letters for more mundane matters of
communication. Moreover, as the magnificent abundance of
triadic utterances in Welsh − and in Irish − suggests, the Druids
and their learned colleagues used these triadic statements as
mnemonics for their sacred traditions. The remarkable Celtic
sensitivity to natural beauty and to the things of nature
expresses itself in the magnificent poetry of, first of all the Irish
bards, the third component of the Druidic orders and later of
medieval Wales. The words used for this tripartite order, which
is found in Europe and in the British Isles, are Gaulish as

recorded by the classics: *Druides* ('priest-philosophers'), *Vates* or *Manteis* ('diviners and prophets'), and the *Bardi* ('panegyric poets'). It is a most noteworthy fact that this threefold category of learned orders is found several centuries later, with the same connotations, in Ireland. It was clearly common to the entire Celtic world and these were the most powerful elements and the most influential in the whole of Celtic society. Indeed, the power of the Druids was so great that the Romans, who spent much time in trying to deprive the Celts of their political and military powers and make them subordinate to the will of Rome, issued an edict, the intention of which was greatly to weaken the *political* influence of the highest order of this trilogy of learned men.

From the above we learn that the Celts, whose society was tribally organised, depended in various ways upon this three-fold group of scholars who had spent, in the case of a Druid – Irish *Druí*; Welsh *Derwydd, Dryw* (the latter also means 'wren', a sacred Druidic bird) – some 20 years in mastering his subject, and thus qualifying to teach his acolytes orally – for the Druids did not use the written word for educational purposes, believing that it weakened the memory. The Druid chanted the lesson and the pupils chanted it back until the seminar was completed and their knowledge considered adequate. Books were no doubt in the possession of the Druids, in Gaul as in Ireland and elsewhere in the Celtic world, but they would have been kept in some secret place, to which the non-initiated would have no access.

It took some 12 years to become a Vatis (Irish *Fáith*; Welsh *Gweledydd*). Poetry was sacred to the Celts and the three degrees of learned men must master the highly complex poetic metres until they were completely facile in their use. The Vates or *Fáith* were also prophets and men of general high learning.

It took seven years of practice in composition to become a Bard (Irish *Bard*; Welsh *Bardd*) who was accredited with great powers of praise and of satire and was thus feared; the functions of the poet and the Druid were very similar in so far as both were skilled in magic. Women, too, could be trained in all three orders and, like the men, were taught the highly secret language known in Irish as *bérla na bfiled*. There is a delightful passage in a medieval Irish tale, which describes the courtship by Cú Chulainn of Emer, daughter of one of the regional kings of Ireland. The young warrior crosses the country in all his finery, his chariot and mettlesome ponies driven by his skilful charioteer, and, knowing the girl's father to be absent, he leaves his charioteer outside the gates, leaps over the ramparts – and finds the only girl he knows is fit to be his wife sitting on the green lawns with her maidens, working at their embroidery. Emer's beauty astonishes Cú Chulainn, and Emer, when she looks up, is amazed by the sight of the youth whose renown and comeliness have often been described to her. He begins to speak to her in *bérla na bfiled*, to which she replies fluently and so they are able to converse about how they can come together. Meanwhile, the girls continue their sewing, comprehending nothing of what is being said.

The Celtic tribe consisted of the King, the men of learning i.e. Druids, Prophets and Bards, the warriors and finally the artisans and craftsmen; the unskilled people were regarded as being of little consequence. Sometimes the King and Druid were one and the same. The Druid had many functions; his training was long and arduous, taking up to 20 years before it was complete; he was fully integrated into Celtic society and had several important rôles, priest, prophet, and very importantly teacher; physician, guardian of the laws and genealogies. The *File* (Welsh *Gweledydd*) was also a prophet and an esoteric poet using, as we know from Old Irish, immensely complicated metrical systems. The third class, the Bards were employed to praise their rulers and to satirize their enemies. They had an unexpectedly important rôle in society, as they were considerably feared. Their praise-poetry was vital to ensure the much-coveted Fame (Irish *clú,* Gaelic *cliú,* Welsh *clod*) to which all rulers aspired, whereas their satire could cause physical blemish or even have the power to bring about the death of the one subjected to it.

The Druids belonged to the élite class of Irish society known as the Aes Dáno, which referred especially to the poets but also to smiths, jurists and the Druids. The Warriors were vital, both for protection and for the land-acquisition of the tribe. The rest of the people consisted of the farmers and the craftsmen but they held a lower place in the Laws. Nevertheless, every member of the tribe, down to the lowest servant or slave, had his or her place within the legal system and had certain rights. The worst punishment that could be meted out to a wrongdoer was to be driven out of the tribal domain into the wilderness where he would become what in early Irish was termed *écland*, i.e. an outcast, without a tribe or clan and therefore entirely devoid of any protection.

The Irish Druids, Fili and Bards were much given to divining the future by means of spells. There were three important methods of performing these rites: *imbas forosna* ('knowledge that enlightens'); *teinm laeda*, which involved offerings to demons and animal sacrifice; *díchetal do chennaib* ('invocation by means of heads'). The earliest known account of *imbas forosna* is given by Bishop Cormac of Cashel in the ninth century. The poet must chew a piece of the raw flesh of a pig, dog or cat which he then offers to his idols. He puts his hands on his cheeks and falls asleep; then the future is revealed to him. Cormac says that St Patrick banned *imbas forosna* and *teinm laeda* because of their pagan character, but did not dislike *díchetal do chennaib*. This suggests that stone heads may have been employed in this period, not human skulls. However, we know that divination was carried out by means of human skulls in the shamanistic traditions of northern Europe and as these were used for many other purposes, both evil-averting and prognostic (see also Chapter 4) we cannot rule out this possibility. The whole process must have been conducted with a high degree of secrecy after the coming of Christianity to the Celtic world.

In spite of their associations with paganism the poets were a wealthy and influential group in possession of considerable and enduring power in Irish society down the ages.

Mogh Ruith: Chief Druid of Ireland and all the World

The name of this eminent pagan character means literally 'Servant of the Wheel'. He was thought to have lived between the first and third centuries AD. Some writers regard him as the Sun-god, because he had only one eye. He figures in the medieval Irish texts as a powerful Druid, and, in common with Druids and Druidism in general, he was capable of marvellous feats and possessed of magical powers. His name derives from the word *roth* ('wheel'). Mogh Ruith allegedly lived to a great age, during which he witnessed the reigns of 19 kings. He was the eponymous ancestor of the tribe of Fir Maige Féne whose name still exists in the barony of Fermoy (*Fir Maige* in Co. Cork). His mother was a young girl brought from Britain as a slave. Mogh Ruith had a splendid chariot of *findruine* ('white bronze' or 'white gold'), set with shining gems. To those who travelled in it night seemed like day. In it he flew through the air like a great bird.

Another enigmatic *roth* or 'wheel' was the magical *Roth Rámach*, 'oared wheel', which is associated with this character elsewhere. Cormac, in his ninth-century Glossary, refers to this wheel as *Roth Fáil* ('the wheel of light', cf. Welsh *gwawl* 'light'). In one of the prophecies attributed to St Columba (Colum Cille) the *Roth Rámach* is described as a huge ship which could sail over both sea and land. A fragment of this wheel was identified with a pillar-stone which was situated at Cleghile, close to the town of Tipperary. It was said to have had such power that it would kill any who laid hands on it, blind those who looked upon it and render deaf those who heard it. Two further details of the tradition of Mogh Ruith may be noted: he was looked upon as the champion of paganism, therefore the enemy of Christianity.

Because of this, some scholarly writers concluded that the euhe-
merized Mogh Ruith had learnt his *Druidheachd* (Druidism or
magic) from Símón Druí (Simon Magus: *Magus* was often used
for *Druid* in the medieval period in Ireland). According to ecclesiastical tradition, Simon Magus was, in a later legend, represented as a formidable opponent of St Peter and he attempted to
demonstrate his superior powers by rising up into the air in a
fiery chariot. Moreover, the belief that the death-dealing pillar-
stone of Cnámchaill was a fragment from the great *roth* or wheel
(*in Roth Rámach*) strengthened the supposition that the Wheel
was itself an instrument of destruction. It was prophesied that the
Roth Rámach would sweep across Europe before Judgment Day as
a punishment for the way in which Simon Magus and others
from every nation had opposed St Peter.

1 Taranis, le Châtelet,
Haute-Marne, France

The cult of the wheel is very well attested in Celtic mythology. There was a major pan-Celtic deity whose name, Taranis, means 'the Thunderer', one of whose most regular attributes was the wheel *(1)*. Votive wheels in bronze or gold have been found widely in Europe and apotropaic jewellery on which the sacred wheel is portrayed is prolific in the Celtic period. Vessels, perhaps for sacred purposes of pottery or metal were also frequently decorated with this most sacred Celtic symbol. The invention of wheeled transport of course obviously revolutionised man's capacity for wider travel; and in the *La Tène* period the new technology of heating the iron and shrinking it onto the wooden felloe rendered the completed artefact infinitely more efficient and durable and allowed greater distances to be covered with less damage to the wheel. The wheel was both a symbolic object (parallels with the sun-disc are obvious), and the attribute of several powerful Celtic deities, as well as being an object of very real practical value in transport, especially after the invention of iron-rimmed tyres.

~⚬ Chapter 1 ⚬~
DRUIDIC ORIGINS

Druidic origins are an integral part of the Celtic society which created them and in which they served as the most learned priests and scholars.

Before considering the nature of the Druidic orders, it will be necessary to glance at the source material. The evidence of archaeology can add validity to the written sources; later the Celtic oral tradition plays its own important rôle. Temporally it is to the Classical authors that we must look, considering, first, the writings of the Greeks and, later, the Latin comments of the Romans the veracity of which cannot always be assumed by reason of the fact that some of their comments were written in their rôle as conquerors. As we know, history tends to be written by the victors.

Nevertheless, in this complex subject every fragment of evidence must be considered. The Greeks were at war with the Celts at an earlier period than the Romans *(2);* however, many of their comments are not concerned with military matters but consist of travellers' tales for, contrary to uninformed opinion, the peoples of Europe and the British Isles travelled over great distances in the last two millennia BC, using ancient trade routes and also embarking upon military expeditions. There may be evidence for direct trade with China, perhaps as early as the late Bronze Age, when bronze votive bird chariots and socketed celts were exchanged amongst other goods for much-coveted Chinese silk and commodities rare in the West.

By the sixth century BC at least, lavish graves of *Hallstatt* Celts were being created in southern Germany and elsewhere, testifying to a strong belief in life after death. This continues in the different but equally important *La Tène* graves, dating to the period of Celtic expansion in Europe. The future, with its ever-more-sophisticated technologies, may reveal more wonders and a broader human picture. Meanwhile, the evidence of archaeology, and the writings about and by the Celts must be our most reliable source material.

In Ireland the concept of the warrior Druid was very highly developed. In opposition to this, the classical commentators on the Gauls convey the impression – indeed, in some cases actually state – that the Druids did not take part in the seemingly perpetual battles and skirmishes of the Gallic warriors. We examine more closely the classical comments on the Druids in Chapter 2 and elsewhere but I should like to point out at this stage that the classics do not actually say that the Druids did not take part in battles, but rather that they were exempt from doing so. This obviously gave them the option of entering the fray, not necessarily by physically fighting with weapons, but certainly – as is attested by the classics and a regular feature of Irish warfare – by exhorting their own side by means of Druidic magic and spells and by adopting ritual postures. In the Irish texts the Druids are described in some instances as encircling the armies, on one leg, with one eye closed and one arm extended (see Ross, A. 2000, fig.26). This magic posture was known as *corrguinecht*, because it appears to have imitated the position adopted by one of the most sacred birds, the crane or *corr*.

It is also an attitude taken by geese. Having possessed six Welsh geese, now reduced to two by the depredations of fox and polecat, I was fascinated to be able to study them closely when they were taking their habitual sleep during daylight hours. Five of them would tuck their heads underneath their wings; the sixth

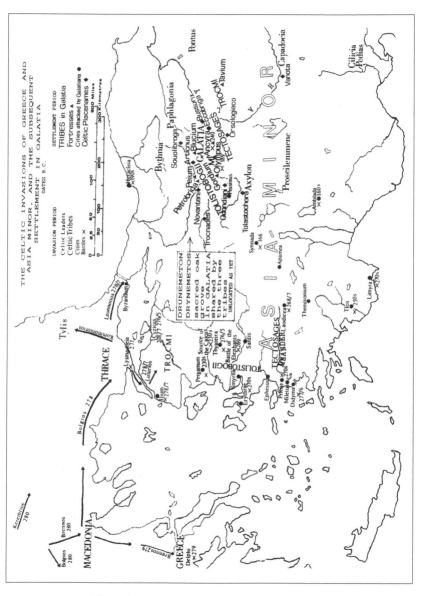

2 The Celtic invasions of Greece and Asia Minor,
and the subsequent settlement in Galatia

would stand on one leg, with one wing outstretched and with one eye open – and even now, rather pathetically, one of the geese will sleep while the other keeps guard as if he were protecting a whole flock. I have always been particularly impressed by the ornithological accuracy, not only of the Celtic and Gallo-Roman artists, but the verbal verisimilitude which indicates an acute observation of birds and the wildlife with which Ireland and the continent of Europe were at that time teeming. This was of course heightened by the fact that the gods and Druids were shape-shifters, according to the tradition, turning themselves or others into bird or animal form while retaining their human reason and power of speech.

Once again, and not for the last time, we must ask the question as to where and how the Celtic world began:

> In a restricted area of East Europe, the occurrence of female figurines in the settlement débris has led to unverifiable assumptions about the cult of a Mother Goddess; in Western Europe, an alien and unknown set of beliefs must have been involved in the building of megalithic or rock-cut collective tombs. We are, in fact, ignorant of what may well have been many varieties of religious experience among the European and Neolithic communities from the sixth to the late third millennium BC and their contribution to later Celtic religion is a wholly unknown factor. ... By the time of the historically documented Druids the background of possible religious tradition would then be roughly as follows. Taking as a starting-point the forms of Celtic religion as inferred from archaeology, epigraphy and the classical and vernacular texts, there are three main antecedent phases. The first would be the traditions, predominantly Indo-European, going back to the second millennium, and perhaps to its beginnings. Behind this again would be the wholly obscure religions of the Neolithic agriculturalists with, in Gaul and especially Britain, eastern and western components mixed from the end of the fourth millen-

nium BC. And finally, underlying all, there would be the beliefs and rites of the hunting peoples of pre-agricultural Europe which might well have contained elements surviving in shamanism. It is a pedigree which could be a good twenty thousand years in length. Druidism, when we first encounter it, is an integral part of the social structure of Celtic Gaul; it is an Indo-European institution with, whatever criticisms may be levelled against the over-elaborate schemes of Dumézil and his school, analogues in the Brahmin class of Sanskrit India or the archaic priesthoods of early Rome. But there are *distinctive* [my emphasis] elements which may owe their existence to those earlier sources of European religious tradition we have just sketched out.

(Piggott 1968, pp.185 and 187)

Without, I hope, appearing to step beyond the bounds of rational surmise, I have recently become much intrigued by Lepenski Vir, a site on the River Danube near a point known as the 'Iron Gates' (Serbia/Romania) *(3)*. Although this remarkable settlement in wild, remote and almost inaccessible landscape, close to the wide reaches of the river, pre-dates the presumptive origins of the Celts by at least two thousand years, I want briefly to consider whether there is any evidence to suggest that it played some rôle as the cradle of Celtic origins. What evidence is there that could possibly justify such a tentative assumption? There are certain features which would seem, perhaps, to point to some sort of link with the much later Celts as we have come to know them. First of all, this settlement, in remote and difficult mountainous terrain, was built on the very verge of the River Danube. *Danube* itself is a Celtic name, as are many of the river names of Europe. It stems from a root *dana* which simply means 'water'. Moreover, it is traditionally the favourite cradle of the Celts for scholars. The king of the tribe – who often was also a Druid – was an immensely powerful figure, but the Druid took precedence even over the king. In the early Irish written tradi-

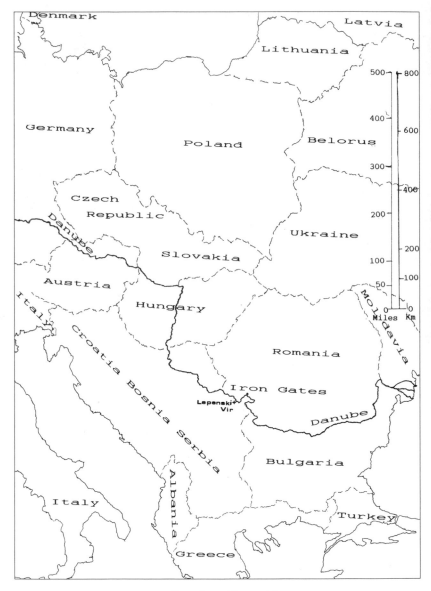

3 Location of Lepenski Vir

tion we learn that: 'no man may speak before the king but the king himself may not speak before the Druid.' The Druids of antiquity *claimed* that their origins and their doctrine were extremely old. They were clearly not thinking in terms of two or three centuries but of perhaps two or three thousand years.

Let us look now at some of the most prevalent of Druidic beliefs and teachings, some of which we have already noted. Relevant here is the universal importance which was accorded to the severed human head – animal heads too were displayed but did not possess quite the same powers. Fire also was a magical and essential focus of cult, and fire festivals at ancient sacred cere-monies have persisted on the same dates as those sacred to the ancient Celtic peoples. The hearth – like the threshold under which sacrificial offerings were often made – was likewise the focus of superstitious belief and worship and this belief has not yet died out in the surviving Celtic areas. In it, the sacred fire burned. Before it, a human head, perhaps of an ancestor was buried – even today in the Celtic lands a human or animal head, often that of the horse was, and perhaps still is, buried under the threshold and under the hearth and often two heads were also built into the upper part of the fireplace. At Lepenski Vir a human jaw (mandible) was found buried in front of the hearth. We may perhaps compare this to the much later central hearth in an Iron Age house excavated in South Uist, Outer Hebrides, Scotland, around which pig jaws had been carefully buried. Ancestor-worship was (and to a certain extent, still may be) therefore a very important aspect of Celtic superstitious belief and at Lepenski Vir, our Neolithic site on the Danube, the impressive finds yielded by expert excavations in the last decade or so are strikingly reminiscent of those of the early Celtic world.

Most noteworthy is the remarkable series of stone heads, the expressive power of which makes a deep and unsettling impact upon the viewer. They are disconcertingly reminiscent of certain, later Celtic carved heads and like them, in spite of the 'human' features, one is reminded of the grim images which are conjured up by the early Irish descriptions of such dark and dangerously magical characters as the Fomorians, against whom the people of Ireland waged war. What stories could these almost sentient heads tell? The similarity to early Celtic stone carvings is further paralleled by the complex carved patterns on the so-called 'altars', reminiscent of the Newgrange style of stone decoration. For the time being the mystery of Lepenski Vir must be borne in mind but much remains to be explained before we can, if ever, link the site to the presumptive Danubian origins of the early Celts.

Or again, did the Celts originate, as some scholars have suggested, in the far West, in Ireland, which was described by Avienus as *Insula Sacra*, the Sacred Isle? There are certainly many indications that this could have been so. The ancient stone-built burial chambers and passage graves which stud the landscape, the hillforts which are now coming to be recognised as ceremonial sites rather than solely as structures for defence; the cult of the human head, the skull or a part of the skull or images of the head in stone and other substances, reveal traces of a great antiquity, as do the complex spiral and meandering decorative carvings on and inside such structures as passage graves, standing stones, lintels and so forth. All this, and much more; the very archaic nature of the Irish language, for example, which was committed to writing at an unusually early period; the prolific and complex nature of the legal system and the rigidly organised structure of Celtic tribal society, must be considered. Most remarkable is perhaps the richness and longevity of the vernacular literature, especially the amazingly complex nature of the poetic metres and the accurate knowledge of time and seasons, special days and periods, the astronomical phenomena, and the fact that they counted their days in nights and called themselves 'sons of the god of night'. The Druids of Gaul are accredited by the classical commentators with having a triad of moral codes which are worthy of the Christian ethic. These, as noted above, are 'Worship the gods, tell the truth, be manly.' Reading through the Irish Triads again recently, I was struck by a very similar triadic dictate: 'Three things that show every good man: a special gift, valour, piety.'

'A special gift' (Irish *dón*) could have one of several connotations: according to Marstrander's *Dictionary of the Irish Language* (1913) it could mean 'a gift, endowment, present ... a divine gift from God [or the gods, presumably] ... a grateful gift is speech without boasting ... in a special sense a latent endowment, faculty, ability ingenium ... skill in applying the principles of a special science ... the art of poetry ... a man versed in a certain art [magic?]'.

Ireland, then is an attractive and perhaps tempting choice for the ultimate place of origin for the complex and highly talented, war-mad peoples whom, for the sake of convenience we term 'the Celts'. Tribally organised, each tribe had its own name which had clearly been bestowed upon it for a good reason; the Morini (sea people) who dwelt on the coastline of what we now call Pas-de-Calais, to name but one example. Whether they all *knew* themselves by this collective term must remain in question. The Greek ethnographers of the second and first centuries BC certainly used the term 'Celt' for the 'barbarians' who lived in the

4 Celtic coins illustrating cauldrons; silver, south Gaul *(left);* gold, Viducasses *(right)*

hinterland to the north and came to pose a constant and terrify-
ing threat to Greek society. They did, however, state categorically
that these people knew themselves as Celts (*Keltoi*). Their religion, with its 'barbaric' cult practices, shows a great homogeneity
throughout the wider 'Celtic' world. Perhaps the most striking of
these, as we have seen, is the veneration which was accorded to
the severed human head. Other objects of veneration were the
cult of ancestors, of graves, of the hearth, fire, certain kinds of
trees and particular animals. The symbol of the cauldron was also
widespread, either portrayed in some medium such as stone or
metal *(4)*, or as an actual, practical vessel *(5 and 6)* for various
sacred or domestic purposes or, in the mythology, as a cult object
possessing its own powers – as did weapons which were believed
to be inhabited by demons. Miniature cauldrons, which were

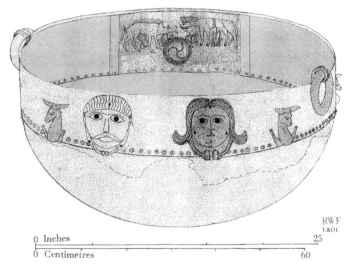

0 Inches   25

0 Centimetres   60

5 Cauldron, Illemose, Rynkeby, Funen, Denmark. Conjectural
reconstruction of the fragmentary cauldron which originally comprised
an upper, cylindrical wall attached by rivets to a round-bottomed
bowl. The second handle, a pair of bulls and a conjectural mask have
been added to the existing remains

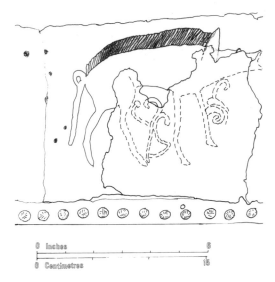

6 Rynkeby cauldron. A third fragment, part of another inner panel, bears the same design of a boar as that which appears on the complete panel

probably of a votive nature, have been recovered from various sites, and recently from a hoard found in Wiltshire (see Stead, 1998). Magical cauldrons also occur in the rich mediaeval literary tradition of Wales and Ireland.

‑ɕ Chapter 2 ɕ‑
THE CLASSICAL COMMENTATORS

W e depend for such knowledge as we have about the Druids and their Order in early Celtic society, on the commentaries of the Greek and Roman writers. These can be used for comparative purposes when we are studying the vernacular writings of the insular Celts, Welsh (Brythonic) – sometimes known as P-Celtic – and especially Gaelic, both Irish and Scottish, the early and medieval Irish texts being the more prolific. This group is known as Goedelic (Q-Celtic). The Irish hagiographies (lives of the saints) contain many mythological elements, and not a few references to the Druids; likewise the early Irish Laws – the oldest laws in Europe in the vernacular – and the Penitentials. Irish poetry and the Metrical Dindshenchas – literally, 'stories about prominent places' – have their own contribution to make to the study, as have the ancient names of places, some of which are discernible in the modern nomenclature. Breton and Welsh literatures and hagiographies are likewise invaluable as source material. The enigmatic Pictish sources have a contribution to make, as do writings in the Ogam script. One of the most rewarding disciplines is that of archaeology in Europe and the British Isles, and this is increasingly the case. As the availability to archaeologists of new technology increases, it is becoming possible to obtain the necessary evidence without inflicting too much damage to a given site.

The earliest teachers

Who then were these Druids? Druidism flourished among the Celts of Gaul where Druidism had a long history, no one as yet knows quite how long; but they themselves believed their order to be very ancient indeed. A good deal of information on Gaulish Druidism is given by Greek and Latin writers from the first century BC. Druidism may have come to Ireland with the coming of the Celts, if indeed they ever 'came', and it was to develop slightly differently from that of Gaul. The chief authors who wrote about the Gaulish Druids are Posidonius (*c.*135–*c.*50 BC); Julius Caesar (102–44 BC); Strabo (63 BC – AD 12 – who is the first to use the term *Vates*); Diodorus Siculus (*floruit* under Julius Caesar and Augustus and lived to at least AD 21); Pomponius Mela (*c.*AD 43) and Lucan (*c.*AD 39-65).

Of these Caesar tells us most, and his account, which we consider in some detail below, is clearly that of a man with a wide knowledge of religion in general. Julius Caesar is famous for, and usually associated with, his successful suppression of Gaul. His comments on the religion of the Gauls are sometimes treated with less respect than is their due, being dismissed as the mere observations of a soldier and brilliant tactician. He was, however, himself a priest of the Imperial Cults of Rome, being one of the 16 *pontifices* of these cults. His ultimate triumph was not perhaps in his conquest of Gaul, but in his election in 63 BC as *pontifex maximus*. It can thus be seen that the particular interest he took in the religious cults of the conquered were not merely observations of a triumphant general but were born of a priest's natural interest in comparative religion. He equates the deities of Gaul with those of other peoples and so provides us with a great deal of interesting information.

The work of Posidonius was probably used by Caesar and other, later writers. These writers all state that the Druids were the learned class of the Gaulish Celts, philosophers and theologians. Pomponius Mela calls them 'teachers of wisdom'. He says they profess to know the size and shape of the world, the movements of the heavens and of the stars, and the will of the gods. (This I think gives us strong proof that they were in fact priests, no matter what else may have been their special concerns.) Caesar seems to substantiate this statement when he says the Druids hold 'many discussions regarding the stars and their movements, the size of the universe and the earth, the order of nature, the strength and the powers of the immortal gods'. Caesar had lived for a long time in Gaul and must have been satisfied that these statements were correct. Strabo says that 'the Druids, in addition to natural philosophy, study also moral philosophy'. Diodorus calls them 'philosophers and *theologians* who are held in much honour'.

The Druids were lawyers and judges, according to Caesar: 'It is they who decide in almost all disputes, public and private, and if any crime has been committed ... or there is any dispute about succession or boundaries, they also decide it, determining rewards and penalties.' Strabo agrees that 'they are entrusted with the decision, not only of private disputes, but of public disputes as well', and adds that 'in former times they even arbitrated in cases of war'.

The Druids are usually represented as having preternatural powers, of divination and prophecy; and of foretelling future events by means of, for example, observing the flight of birds – augury. The oak was the most venerated of trees *(7)*.

Timagenes, a Greek historian from Alexandria, writing in the first century BC, mentions the Druids' searchings into 'secret and sublime things'. Cicero states that Diviciacus, chief of the Aedui and a close friend of Caesar, was a Druid and 'given to the practice of divination'. In the first century AD Tacitus represents the British Druids as encouraging their people to resist the Romans 'with the prophetic utterances of an idle superstition'. Dio Chrysostom, moreover, says that the Druids 'concern themselves with divination and all branches of wisdom'. Caesar speaks of the Druids as an organised body. The Druids are often thought of as magicians with powers of transforming the things of nature into the appearance of something quite different. This power seems not to have been

7 An oak tree and acorns

alluded to by the earlier writers. Pliny is the first to emphasise it and he is followed by later writers. Of the mistletoe ceremony he says 'They believe that the mistletoe, taken in drink, imparts fecundity to barren animals and that it is an antidote to all poisons.' He describes herbs that must be gathered in a certain way, on the sixth day of the moon. '... [F]or it is by the moon that they measure their months and years, and also their ages of thirty years'. These 'protect both men and cattle from every kind of evil.' His most remarkable story is that of the serpent's egg which must only be caught in a cloak and may be tested 'by seeing if it floats against the current of a river even though it be set in gold'. Pliny claims to have seen a specimen of this egg which 'is said to ensure success in law-suits and a favourable reception with princes'. Pliny alone gives details of the magical power of the Druids but Hippolytus and others do mention them. He says in the early third century that the Druids are 'seers, prophets and magicians'. Almost all the early writers comment that the central teaching of the Druids was the *immortality* of the soul.

Caesar says the Druids imparted knowledge not only to their own acolytes but to others. They were also exempt from taxation and military service.

> Tempted by these great rewards, many young men assemble of their own accord to receive their training, many are sent by friends and relations. Report says that in the schools of the Druids they learn by heart a great number of verses, and therefore some persons remain twenty years under training.
>
> (*De Bello Gallico*.VI 14)

In the mid-first century AD Pomponius Mela (*De Situ Orbis*, III, 2, 18, 19) says 'They teach many things to the nobles of Gaul in a course of instruction lasting as long as twenty years, meeting in secret either in a cave or in a secluded dale.'

The teachings of the Druids comprised both natural and moral philosophy, the nature of the universe and of the gods. Little is known of their secular teaching, but almost all who have written about them declare that their central moral teaching was the immortality of the soul. Caesar states that the cardinal doctrine which they seek to teach is that souls do not die, but after death *pass from one to another*.

Strabo says they assert 'that men's souls and also the universe are indestructible'. Pomponius Mela has it that 'one of their dogmas has come to common knowledge, namely, that souls are eternal and there is another life in the infernal regions'. Earlier writers simply state that the Druids believe in the immortality of the soul. Later writers claim that this immortality involved transmigration. Diodorus Siculus, writing *c*.8 BC says 'The Pythagorean doctrine prevails among them (the Gauls), teaching that the souls of men are immortal and live again for a fixed number of years in another body.' Lucan, writing in the early first century AD, addresses the Druids thus: 'And it is you who say that the shades of the dead seek not the silent land of Erebus, and the pale halls of Pluto; rather, you tell us that the same spirit has a body again elsewhere, and that death, if what you sing is true, is but the mid-point of long life.' An important remark by Diogenes Laertius *(Lives of the Philosophers),* writing in the third century AD, states: 'the Druids make their pronouncements by means of riddles and dark sayings, teaching that the gods must be worshipped, and no evil done, and manly behaviour maintained', that is: 'worship the gods, do no evil, be manly'.

Caesar is the only classical source who provides information about the actual teaching of the Druids. What he has to say is confirmed by Origen, writing in the third century AD, who comments that nothing survives of their writings. (We now know, as more and more important inscriptions come to light, that this is not strictly true.) But Caesar says:

> And they do not think it proper to commit these utterances to writing, although in almost all other matters, and in their public and private accounts, they make use of Greek letters. I believe they have adopted the practice for two reasons – that they do not wish the rule to become public property, nor those who learn the rule to rely on writing and so neglect the cultivation of the memory; and in fact, it does usually happen that the assistance of writing tends to relax the diligence of the student and the action of the memory
>
> *(De Bello Gallico)*

Pliny is a very valuable informant about Druidism in Gaul and he provides welcome testimony which would seem to imply that Druidism originated in Britain and spread across the sea to other regions. He says *(Nat. Hist,* XXX, 13):

It (magic) flourished in the Gallic provinces, too, even down to a period within our memory; for it was in the time of the Emperor Tiberius that a decree was issued against the Druids and the whole tribe of diviners and physicians. But why mention all this about a practice that has even crossed the ocean and penetrated to the utmost parts of the earth? At the present day, *Britannia* [my emphasis] is still fascinated by magic, and performs its rites with so much ceremony that it almost seems as though it was she who had imparted the cult to the Persians. To such a degree do people throughout the whole world, although unlike and quite unknown to one another, agree upon this one point. ...

In 55 and 54 BC Julius Caesar attacked Britain and made some impression upon the southern tribes. After nearly a century, a more serious invasion was led by Claudius in AD 43, and the country was more or less subdued by the Romans in the richer south. The process of Romanising Britain proceeded fairly swiftly in the more civilised tribal areas, and with considerable difficulty as they moved further north. The famous – or infamous – attack by the Romans on the rich tribe of the Iceni (or Eceni) of East Anglia *(plate 1)*, the killing of the powerful queen Boudica's husband Prasutagos, the raping and flogging of her two daughters and the flogging of Boudica herself – her name means 'victory' and is current yet in the contemporary Welsh female name *Buddug* – led to violent retaliation. In AD 60-61 the inflamed Icenian queen led a furious revolt against the hated invaders. They razed to the ground Colchester (then *Camulodunum*, 'fort of the god Camulos'), London *(Londinium)*; then St Albans *(Verulamium)*, and killed an estimated 80,000 people before Boudica was defeated. She took poison and so ended her life.

But before setting out for Colchester, she invoked her powerful goddess Andraste and, as she was a priestess and thus probably a Druidess, she released a hare, reading the omens from the course it took, which were, apparently, auspicious. The Romans particularly hated the powerful priestess-queen for the terrible vengeance she wreaked upon the helpless Roman women, who had been left unprotected. In her sacred grove *(nemeton)*, she and her warriors impaled them before hanging them in the trees, cutting off their breasts and stuffing them into their mouths to make it appear that they were eating them. She had her revenge, and a very violent one at that. Later in the same year, the Roman army, before the winter set in, pressed northwards under the leadership of Paulinus, heading for Môn (Anglesey), which was a centre of British Druidism. Tacitus (*Annals*, XIV, 30) provides an equally graphic account of the Roman campaign against Môn:

> On the shore stood the opposing army with its dense array of armed warriors while between the ranks dashed women in black attire like the Furies, with hair dishevelled, waving brands. All around, the Druids, lifting up their hands to heaven and pouring forth dreadful imprecations, scared our soldiers by the unfamiliar sight, so that, as if their limbs were paralysed, they stood motionless and exposed to wounds. Then urged by their general's appeal and mutual encouragements not to quail before a troop of frenzied women, they bore the standards onwards, smote down all resistance, and wrapped the foe in the flames of his own brands. A force was next set over the conquered, and their groves, devoted to inhuman superstitions, were destroyed. They deemed it, indeed, a duty to cover their altars with the blood of captives and to consult their deities through human entrails.

It seems likely that Penmon, which overlooks the Menai Straits and is heavily wooded today, is the site of this gory encounter, in which Irish as well as British Druids may well have united to protect the sacred island from their Roman enemies, so hostile to their religion. It is noteworthy that some 20 miles north-west, lies a small lake, Llyn Cerrig Bach ('the Lake of the Small Stones'). It was at this site, some 5 miles south-east of Holyhead, that an airfield was constructed. In 1942, peat from the boggy ground of this lake-studded area was required in the preparation of the landing strip at Valley. During the work, some metal objects, together with animal bones, were found by workmen on the site. Archaeologist Sir Cyril Fox first visited the site in August 1943, and by chance picked up a currency bar. It is admirable to learn that the workmen had been told to pick up every metal object they saw. We cannot go into the whole story in this context, but as the runway was urgently required, archaeologists had only a very limited time in which to excavate the site and it is very likely that artefacts remained un-reclaimed in the area or in the clay or peat or overhanging rock. It was hoped that future scientific examination might be possible, but so far this has not taken place. The site is of great importance to our theme, as the huge amount of deposits, mostly of metalwork, recovered made it quite clear that this was a ritual lake and bog area, into which offerings of very high quality – metalwork from all over the British Isles, and great quantities of bone – had been deposited. It is thought to be likely that Llyn Cerrig Bach and the surrounding area of boggy land had been a sacred offer-place for an unknown length of time. News of the terrible events surrounding Boudica's destruction of Londinium – her violent death by her own hand, and the triumph of the Romans, who were then on the march northwards – must have reached Môn, which was the centre of British Druidism, and consequently Druids would have come from far and wide, including Ireland (Irish metalwork was found amongst the hoard, also from north Britain). There was a huge quantity, then, of metalwork, and that which could be retrieved was subjected to analysis and is now in the National Museum of Wales, Cardiff. The archaeologists had, of necessity, to concentrate upon manufactured articles, and although great quantities of bones were unearthed, there was no opportunity to preserve these, or to study them in detail. Thus, although human and animal sacrifice are extremely likely to have taken place on some scale in such a crisis, it has not yet been possible to confirm this.

During this terrible time in early British history (mid-first century AD) human sacrifices must have been widely offered on a lavish scale. Apart from Llyn Cerrig Bach, which would almost certainly have been one of these sites, there are other sacred lakes and peat bogs in Wales, Cheshire and throughout the British Isles which are likely to have been offer-sites into which gifts – including sacrificed human beings – would have been made to the uncaring gods. Môn, moreover, has a great number of stone heads, some of probable Iron Age date; sometimes these have been found built, face inwards, into churches. One head, probably of Iron Age date, is situated some 10 miles south-west of Penmon, and when I saw it, was standing on a farm wall and taken down from time to time for ritual purposes. It has a deep 'cigarette-hole' in the corner of its mouth – a feature found on many Iron Age heads, and a quizzical expression *(8)*. It is still the object of veneration, and of rites which have a long ancestry, according to its guardian.

RWF

| 0 Inches | 6 |
| 0 Centimetres | 15 |

8 Stone head, Hendy, Anglesey; with 'cigarette' hole

Ausonius

Decimus Magnus Ausonius was born *c*.AD 310. His life spanned almost the whole of the fourth century. It was a remarkable period of peace and opportunity for pursuit of learning and all matters connected with the intellect. His father, Julius Ausonius, was a doctor, a physician of considerable skill and talent, who, interestingly, could never master the Latin tongue. Presumably he spoke in Gaulish and Greek. He was born in Bazas and settled in Bordeaux, where he practised medicine and where his son, Decimus Magnus, was born. His mother seems not to have been very close to him, but his father he held in very great affection and his subsequent death dealt him a severe blow. Ausonius was highly educated in Bordeaux in Greek and Latin language and literature. Greek he did not like, although his excellent tutors soon overcame his aversion. Around 320 he was sent to live with his maternal uncle, a professor at Toulouse, and there he remained until his uncle was called to Constantinople in about 328 to become tutor to one of the sons of Constantine. The boy then returned to Bordeaux to continue his studies in rhetoric. One of his tutors, it seems, was Delphidius, 'the ill-starred son of the ex-priest of Belenus [*sic*] *and a descendant of the old Druids*' [my emphasis].

Two others were also thus descended: Attius Patera, from the Druids of Bayeux; and Phoebicius, keeper of the temple of Belenos, from the Druids of Armorica (Brittany). Of further interest is the fact that Ausonius' aunt was called *Dryadia*, as was his sister. This would seem to indicate that references to Druidesses (the word *Dryad* means 'Druidess'), as well as to Druids, continued to be used, and without opprobrium. Moreover, two other Gaulish writers who lived about AD 300, just before the birth of Ausonius, were Lampridius and Vopiscus, who provide slight but interesting information about the survival of remnants of Druidism in Gaul at this late period. Lampridius, in a passage relating to the year 235, when Alexander Severus was leaving on an expedition, says of Alexander: 'While he was on his way, a Druidess cried out to him in the Gallic tongue, "Go forward, but hope not for victory, nor put trust in thy soldiers'".Vopiscus likewise refers to the prophecy of a Druidess in the second half of the third century:

> When Diocletian, so my grandfather told me, was sojourning in a tavern in the land of the Tongri in Gaul, at the time he was still of humble rank in the army, and had occasion to settle the daily account for his keep with a certain Druidess, this woman said to him, 'You are far too greedy, and far too economical, O Diocletian.'Whereto he replied, jestingly, 'I will be more liberal when I am emperor', to which the Druidess answered, 'Laugh not, Diocletian, for when you have killed the Boar you will indeed be emperor'. After this, Diocletian coveted the purple, and never missed the chance of killing a boar when out hunting *(plate 4)*; but Aurelian, and Probus, and Tacitus, and then Carus, were all emperors before him, so that he was moved to exclaim, 'I kill the boars, but it is always another who reaps the reward!' At last, however, he killed the præfect, Arrius, surnamed The Boar, and then the prophecy of the Druidess was fulfilled, and he ascended to the imperial throne.

Vopiscus also relates another Druidical prophecy that was made in the reign of Aurelian (AD 270–5).

> He (Asclepiodotus) used to say that on a certain occasion Aurelian consulted the Gaulish Druidesses to find out whether his descendants would remain in possession of the imperial crown. These women told him that no name would become more illustrious in the state annals than that of the line of Claudius. It is true, of course, that the present Emperor Constantius is of the same stock, and I think that his descendants will assuredly attain to the glory foretold by the Druidesses.

These passages are from the works of early classical writers in the post-Druidic period (i.e. after Tiberius' suppression of the Druids

of Gaul in AD 21). However, they were not destroyed, but continued to practise in caves and remote places. In AD 54 Claudius abol-
ished the whole Order, yet in AD 71, in the revolt of Civilis, we find
that Druids were prophesying the destruction of Roman power,
which was portended by a fire which broke out on the Capitol.
Their survival, at this point and beyond, continued, but they seemingly ceased to have the influence which their former teaching of
the offspring of the nobility had given them. Nevertheless, they
were still of use to the upper classes, could help to stir up revolts
and impress by their powers of prophecy and spells and as we have
seen from later sources, the Druidesses did not seem to have
attracted the same opprobrium as did the Druids. There is no question of there being female Druids and in Ireland, at any rate, they
played an active rôle in influencing the nobles and prophesying the
outcome of battles. We know from the classical period that islands
off the shores of Gaul (including Armorica) and Britain, were
inhabited by 'holy women', presumably Druidesses, as were they
by Druids themselves.

Ausonius began his professional career about AD 334, as *gram-
maticus* at the University of Bordeaux. He died *c*.393-4, over 80
years of age. He thus had the inimitable privilege of living in a
Gaul in which the wars with Rome were but a distant memory,
and died very shortly before the barbarian hordes crossed the
frozen Rhine on New Year's Day in 403, and turned Gaul into a
blazing desert. Ireland came to the rescue, attracting scholars who
were threatened by this terrible incursion and, by giving them
lodgings and hospitality, the use of *scriptoria* and peace in a most
beautiful landscape, ensuring the preservation in some measure of
the arts of grammar, rhetoric and other forms of composition
which were so highly developed at this time in Gaul.

Something must be said about Ausonius' attitude towards
Christianity. When and how he adopted the new religion there is
nothing to show; but certain of his poems make it clear that he
professed and called himself a Christian; others revealing a fairly
extensive knowledge of the Scriptures, sometimes lead the unwary

to assume that Ausonius was a devout and pious soul. But in these poems, he is deliberately airing his Christianity. He has, so to speak, 'dressed himself for church'. His everyday attitude was clearly very different. When Paulinus begins to conform his life to what he believed to be the demands of Christianity, Ausonius is totally unable to understand his friend's attitude, and can only believe that he is crazed. Nor does Christianity enter directly or indirectly into the general body of his literary work. In his *Parentalia*, there is no trace of Christian sentiment – and this though he is writing of his nearest and dearest: the rite which gives a title to the book is pagan, the dead 'rejoice to hear their names pronounced'. Ausonius certainly regards a future existence as problematical. Further, the conception of the Dead held by Ausonius was distinctly peculiar – as his less guarded references show. The Trinity is a power transcending, but not unlike the Three Emperors ... for our author, the Christian Deity was not essentially different from the old pagan gods.

If we glance at a passage in *The Daily Round*, called *The Interlude*, we get a better idea of his dual attitude. Here Ausonius prepares to make his morning prayers in his chapel:

Hi, boy! Get up! Bring me my slippers and my tunic of lawn; bring all the clothes that you have ready now for my going out. Fetch me spring water to wash my hands and mouth and eyes. Get me the chapel opened, but with no outward display: holy words and guiltless prayers are furniture enough for worship. I do not call for incense to be burnt, not for any slice of honey-cake; hearths of green turf I leave for the altars of the pagan gods.

This is followed by *The Prayer:*

Grant me, O Father, the effluence of everlasting light for which I yearn, *if I swear not by gods of stone* [my emphasis].

In this charming prayer, by saying what he will not do, he perhaps reveals the temptation to do these very things; be that as it may, Ausonius does give us interesting information about the nature of worship of the pagan gods by mentioning 'hearths of green turf' and altars, which a later part of the prayer tells us are of stone. He also mentions honey cake and the burning of incense. Perhaps the most interesting detail of paganism is the swearing on gods of stone. Bordeaux (*Burdigala*) was a rich Gallo-Roman town and it and the wider district possessed a wealth of pagan carvings portraying 'gods of stone'. These must represent a very small fragment of the originally rich *corpus* of stone carvings displayed in temples and public buildings in this prosperous region.

In the museum of Bordeaux is a splendid stone tricephalus *(plate 2)*, heavily bearded, moustaches drooping in the Celtic fashion, wearing a fine torc. The features of the three faces reveal a strength and proud arrogance typical of some of the portraits of the Celtic warriors themselves. Originally from Condat, Cantal, this superb sculpture was brought to Bordeaux in 1899 – too late, of course, for Ausonius to have seen it! But his 'gods of stone' were no doubt similarly impressive and one can understand the inner conflict that must have taken place in those who turned their backs on these, their time-honoured protectors, for the new faith of Christianity.

Nature poetry was one of the great delights and achievements of the early Irish poets and this genre persisted down the centuries in all its sensitivity and delight in description and detail. It is thus remarkable to find that, amongst his many other enviable talents, Ausonius was a fine nature poet and his remarkable work entitled *Mosella* ('the Moselle') is fully worthy of Irish poetry at its most eloquent and elegant. It is a substantial work and is too long to quote. I should like however to draw attention to some of the loving details with which he describes the ever-changing scene in his journey. The prose translation (White 1968) inevitably loses some of the impact of the original Latin:

Thence onward, I began a lonely journey through a pathless forest. I passed Dumnissus, watered by its unfailing spring, and the lands, lately parcelled out to Sarmatian settlers. At length, on the very verge of Belgic territory, I descry *Noviomagus* (Noyon, Oise), the famed camp of sainted Constantine. Clearer the air which here invests the plains, and Phoebus, cloudless now, discloses glowing heaven with his untroubled light. No longer is the sky to seek, shut out by the green gloom of branches inter-twined: but the free breath of transparent day withholds not sight of the sun's pure rays and of the Aether, dazzling to the eyes. Nay more, the whole gracious prospect made me behold a picture of my own native land, the smiling and well-tended country of Bordeaux – the roofs of country houses, perched high upon the overhanging river banks, the hill-sides green with vines, and the pleasant stream of Moselle gliding below with pleasant subdued murmuring ... Then through thy smooth surface showed all the treasures of thy crystal depths, a river keeping naught concealed: and as the calm air lies open to our gaze, and the stilled winds do not forbid the sight to travel through the void, if our gaze pene-trates thy gulfs, we behold things whelmed far below, and the recesses of thy secret depth lie open ... down beneath their native streams the tossing plants endure the water's buffetting, pebbles gleam and are hid, and gravel picks out patches of green moss ... As the whole Caledonian shore spreads open to the Briton's gaze, when ebbing tides lay bare green seaweed and red coral and whitening pearls, the seed of shells, man's gauds, and under the enriched waves mimic necklaces, counterfeit our fashions; even so, beneath the glad waters of still Moselle weeds of different hue reveal the pebbles scattered amidst them.

Writing in early Medieval Ireland: Ogam

The origins of the Ogam alphabet are obscure; it was, however, in existence in the fifth century as a script for inscriptions on stone or

9 Ogam script, arranged alphabetically and by design

wood. Its distribution in Ireland suggests it may have originated in the south and it is clear that it was created specifically for the Irish language. It may have come into existence in this part of Ireland by the fourth century AD. The originators of the script were clearly familiar with the Latin alphabet but to date we know little about its early history. Originally, the Ogam script consisted of 20 characters divided into four groups of five characters *(9)*. At some stage a fifth group of letters was added.

Some scholars have regarded Ogam as essentially a sign language for use, perhaps by the Druids who kept their sacred learning and poetry a closely guarded secret. It is to be noted that stones bearing inscriptions in Ogam were often 'sanctified' by the addition of a cross, in the post-pagan period. Every vowel and consonant in Ogam possessed a name which allegedly associated each letter with some tree or plant.

Another version of the origin of Ogam is contained in *In Lebor Ogaim*, a tract dealing exclusively with Ogam, and with the

Bríatharogam, both dating from the Old Irish period. In this text, the invention of Ogam is attributed to the god Ogma mac Elathan who was famed for eloquence in speech and poetry and creating the system in order to demonstrate his intellectual powers. His intention was that the alphabet should be reserved for the learned members of society 'to the exclusion of rustics and fools'. According to this school of thought, the first thing ever to be written in Ogam was a message inscribed on a single rod cut from a birch tree, which conveyed a warning to the god Lugh mac Ethlenn: 'Your wife will be carried away from you seven times to the *síd* [the Otherworld] unless the birch should protect her, and this is why *Beithe* [birch] is the first letter in the alphabet, because it was first written on birch.'

The supposition that Ogma invented the Ogam script would seem to be substantiated by the well-known account of the poet Lucian of *Samosate* (born *c.*AD 120). The modern name is *Samsât*; it was a fortified city on the right bank of the Euphrates. Lucian was fluent in Greek and he lectured on the art of rhetoric as far afield as Gaul so we may assume that the scene he describes is based on actual experience. He refers to a representation of the Gaulish god Ogmios (perhaps identical to the Irish Ogma) in the guise of Hercules i.e. wearing a lion's skin and carrying a club, a bow and a quiver. He figures as an old, bald-headed man followed by an eager crowd whose ears were fastened to chains which were in turn attached to his tongue. The significance of this scene was beyond his understanding until a highly educated Gaul, speaking in Greek, explained that the Gauls equated Hercules, not Hermes, with eloquence because the capacity for elegant speech improves with age. This explanation made it at once clear to the stranger that the chains were not intended to portray captive people being dragged along against their will by the god Ogmios but were freely follow-ing him, hypnotised by his eloquence, literally hanging onto his every word.

Early Irish literature contains numerous references to Ogam. The script was used primarily for commemorative inscriptions engraved on stone which were then set up above the resting-places of the deceased. Presumably the Druids played a major rôle in these funerary ceremonies, although there is not a great deal of detailed information on this topic. One example, however, occurs in the Irish *Táin*. The young hero, Cú Chulainn, who is highly-educated as one would expect of a young Celtic nobleman, writes an inscription in Ogam on the peg of a twisted branch, thus creating a ring, and throws it over a standing stone so that he might delay the advance of the enemy – Queen Medb and her army – to Ulster, and give him time for a romantic interlude. Medb's two scouts first come upon the message thrown over the top of the stone, and they observe that Cú Chulainn's horses have been grazing there. Then the army of Connacht comes to the place and the Ogam-inscribed branch is given to Fergus to interpret for them. He reads it as saying 'Let no one go past until there be found a man to throw a withe made from one branch as it is in the same way with one hand. But I except my friend Fergus.' Fergus hands the withe to the Druids and asks them to interpret its 'secret meaning'. They do so, but find nothing different from that which is already known.

Ogam inscriptions had a practical use in Early Irish law. Ogams in stone were used to mark boundaries and entitlement to land. Territorial boundaries were designated by pillar-stones. Ogam thus has funerary associations and functions as burials often took place on boundaries.

Writing and early Christianity in Ireland

The alphabet used in Ireland from the sixth century onwards is the Roman alphabet modified. This was due to the Christian missionaries who accompanied St Patrick. It seems that some Christians were in Ireland before Patrick's time and they probably brought a version of writing with them. One, Pelagius, was of Irish descent although not born in Ireland. Another, Sedulius, may have been an

Irishman, but pursued his studies in Gaul. An incident in the Tripartite Life of Patrick suggests there was writing in pre-Christian Ireland. Pelagius taught at Rome *c.*400, and Sedulius lived in about the first half of the fifth century. In the Tripartite Life, the pagan king Loegaire proposed that the *books* of the Druid Lucatmael and those of Patrick should be cast into water or fire and their truth tested by their escaping unscathed. This would seem to suggest that at this time the Druids *did* have books of some kind. When 'at a later date St Patrick determined upon revising the *Brehon law code*, the books in which it was written were laid before him ... [E]vil laws were cast forth from them and the proper ones arranged.'

Whether or not the Druids had the art of writing in the pre-Patrician days, their *teaching* was largely, if not entirely, oral. The Ogam script could not have been used for long communications. If there was any system of writing prior to Ogam and Latin, there is no evidence, to date, of it. But we cannot deny the possibility of it having existed.

Chapter 3

QUESTIONABLE DEATH AND UNUSUAL BURIAL

The rite of human sacrifice has always been believed to have been carried out under the auspices of the Druids – without whose presence no sacrifice could be offered to the gods – and this is given as the main reason why the Romans were so particularly hostile to the Druidic priesthood. In the first instance, sacrifice, both human and animal, was widely practised in the pre-Christian world. Although human sacrifice had allegedly been abandoned by the Romans some hundred years before the conquest, they nevertheless enjoyed bloodshed and killings, as the ghastly gladiatorial contests and the throwing of human beings to the lions and other wild beasts demonstrates. Indeed, human sacrifices were almost humane in comparison with the appalling atrocities committed by the Romans against the conquered Gauls during their campaign in the first half of the first century BC. The victim of human sacrifice was at least an honoured offering to the gods, whereas often the enemies of the Romans, upon whom vicious injuries had been inflicted, were left to die in pitiless circumstances. For example, we have descriptions of the habit of cutting off the hands and feet of the captured Gauls; they were then thrown into deep ditches and left under the heat of the summer sun to die. As the classical writers themselves constantly commented upon the huge size and strength of their enemies, it is not pleasant to dwell upon the length of time they would have taken before death showed more mercy than the conquerors.

However, there can be no doubt that human and animal sacrifices were carried out by all the Celts of whom we have records.
It is not possible here to go into all the classical writings but we
must give some impression of the forms this rite may have taken.
There were three great Gaulish gods: Teutates ('god of the people
or tribes'), Taranis ('the Thunderer') *(1)*, Esus ('Lord, Master') *(10)*.
These names are found widely in Celtic lands and some have
entered the everyday nomenclature of the Celtic speaking
peoples. Sacrifices were allegedly made to Teutates by drowning,
to Taranis by burning and to Esus by hanging (from a tree) and by
wounding. It is clearly in memory of such threefold sacrifices
that the later Celtic motif of the Threefold Death originates. It is
an ancient concept and one known widely throughout the early

10 Esus felling a tree; above him,
Tarvos Trigaranus a bull with three
cranes. Trier/Trèves, Germany

Indo-European world. Although prisoners and malefactors were the usual victims of sacrifice, on occasion the innocent were also offered to the gods. Caesar comments (*De Bello Gallico*, V, 6, 13) that the Druids:

> have the right to decide nearly all public and private disputes and they also pass judgment and decide rewards and penalties in criminal and murder cases and in disputes concerning legacies and boundaries. When a private person or a tribe disobeys their ruling they ban them from attending at sacrifices. That is their harshest penalty. Men placed under this ban are treated as impious wretches; all avoid them, fleeing their company and conversation, lest their contact bring misfortune upon them; they are denied legal rights and can hold no official dignity. The Druids have one at their head who holds chief authority among them.

and also:

> The whole Gallic people is exceedingly given to religious superstition. Therefore those who are suffering from serious illness or are in the midst of the dangers of battle, either put to death human beings as sacrificial victims or take a vow to do so, and the Druids take part in these sacrifices; for they believe that unless one human life is given in exchange for another human life the power of the almighty gods cannot be appeased. Sacrifices of this kind are also offered for the needs of the state. Some tribes build enormous images with limbs of interwoven branches which they then fill with live men; the images are set alight and the men die in a sea of flame. They believe that the immortal gods delight more in the slaughter of those taken in theft or brigandage or some crime, but when the supply of that kind runs short they descend even to the sacrifice of the innocent.
>
> (*De Bello Gallico*, V, 6, 16)

It is an important fact that, although the Druids officiated at sacrifices, and taught the philosophy of their religion, their position was much more complex than that of authority in religious matters. They held an annual meeting in the region of Chartres and people came from far and wide to have their quarrels and disputes considered and legally tried. The Druids were trained lawyers and highly reputed teachers, as well as being competent in many other disciplines, over and above that of religion. Nevertheless, they held an unassailable authority in this sphere, which was of such great importance to all the Celts. Matters of national concern, such as inter-tribal quarrels, were brought to their council for consideration and adjudication. The fact that they held *national* assemblies and were under the authority of an Archdruid, who was invested with supreme power, makes very clear the fact that their religious system and their total authority were nationally rather than tribally organised. They were the chief instructors of the young, and had a formidable religious sanction behind their decrees. This gives us some idea of their power and control over civil administration and how deeply the enemies of Gaul resented and probably feared their Order. Cicero makes a reference to the Druids and Kendrick says of this:

> It is peculiarly important in this matter of the political prestige of the Druids, because we happen to know something about the particular Druid to whom Cicero (*De Divinatione*, I. xli. 90) refers: 'Nor is the practice of divination disregarded, even among uncivilised tribes, if indeed there are Druids in Gaul – and there are, for I knew one of them myself, Divitiacus [sic], the Æduan, your guest and eulogist. He claimed to have that knowledge of nature, which the Greeks call "physiologia", and he used to make predictions, sometimes by means of augury, and sometimes by means of conjecture.'

Diviciacus the Druid was a statesman, the acknowledged ruler of the Ædui, and a politician and diplomat of high reputation throughout Gaul; Kendrick remarks that Diviciacus was an early example of the great political priests of history. Referring to the paragraph quoted above, Kendrick (1927) writes:

> This, in conjunction with Caesar's testimony, throws a flood of light on the conditions of service in the priesthood during the first century before Christ, and at once disposes of the quite natural idea that all its members were secluded and mysterious ancients, holding aloof from the common world in a gloomy atmosphere of esoteric ritual and priestly taboos. For Divitiacus was a man of affairs, acknowledged ruler of the Ædui, and a politician and diplomat of established reputation throughout the whole of Gaul; it was, in fact, an important diplomatic mission that took him to Rome on the occasion when he was the guest of Quintus Cicero and discussed divination with Tully ... Caesar's own account describes a trusted Keltic nobleman, sagacious in strategy and eloquent in debate, who was incessantly occupied in the difficult domestic problems of Gaul; and when we add to this picture Cicero's testimony as to his religious calling and to his knowledge of Druidic lore and methods of augury, we seem to find ourselves confronted in this man with a forerunner of the great political priests of history. At any rate, we are compelled to enlarge our ideas of the Druidic functions, so as to include the practical administration of government with the necessary complete liberty of movement and freedom in priestly duties.

The end came soon afterwards, though. The country itself was divided, some opposing and some allying themselves to Caesar. The Druidic Order was divided against itself, and this state of anarchy dealt a blow to its authority from which it never recovered. The authority of the Archdruid ceased; the national assembly fell apart and the real power of the Druids was destroyed. This was a complete disaster for Druidic authority from which it never recovered and from then on their significance as a *political*

force was terminated in Gaul. Diodorus Siculus, who wrote *c.*8
BC, makes this clear; and they would now seem to be generally
regarded as prophets and seers.

> When they attempt divination upon important matters they
> practise a strange and incredible custom, for they kill a man by
> a knife-stab in the region above the midriff, and after his fall
> they foretell the future by the convulsions of his limbs and the
> pouring of his blood, a form of divination in which they have
> full confidence, as it is of old tradition. It is a custom of the
> Gauls that no one performs a sacrifice without the assistance
> of a philosopher [Druid], for they say that offerings to the gods
> ought only to be made through the mediation of these men,
> who are learned in the divine nature and, so to speak, familiar
> with it, and it is through their agency that the blessings of the
> gods should properly be sought.
>
> (*Histories*, V, 31, 2-5)

Other information comes from Strabo and Suetonius:

> But the Romans put a stop to these customs, as well as to all
> those connected with the sacrifices and divinations that are
> opposed to our usages. They used to strike a human being,
> devoted to death, in the back with a sabre, and then divine
> from his death-struggle. But they would not sacrifice without
> the Druids. We are told of still other kinds of human sacrifices;
> for example they would shoot victims to death with arrows, or
> impale them in the temples, or having devised a colossus of
> straw and wood, throw into the colossus cattle, and wild
> animals of all sorts, and human beings, and then make a burnt
> offering of the whole thing.
>
> (Strabo, *Geographica*, IV, 4, *c.*198, 5)

He (the Emperor Claudius) very thoroughly suppressed the
barbarous and inhuman religion of the Druids in Gaul, which

in the time of Augustus had merely been forbidden to Roman citizens.

(Suetonius, *Claudius*, 25)

Archaeology presents inevitable problems in this sphere. Human remains are found widely in excavations, many in circumstances which would seem to be only explicable in terms of sacrifice, but that conclusion is not, of course, infallible. There could be many other reasons for death, including murder, death in the single combat which was so much a feature of Celtic life and warfare, and so on. When there would seem to be no remaining traces of ritual activity, death could have been brought about by accident, for example, by getting caught and drowned in a peat bog, falling from some cliff or other height, or becoming lost and dying from starvation. The possibilities are endless. However, the fact that we do know a great deal about the practice from the classical writers does make the possibility of sacrifice at least an option for consideration.

Archaeology then perhaps poses the greatest number of problems in this field. Unless there is any convincing documentary evidence, or even that of folklore, one has to be very wary indeed of jumping too hastily to conclusions. That said, more and more evidence to support the rite of human sacrifice is coming to light as archaeological techniques are becoming vastly more sophisticated and technology in general advances at ever-increasing speed. Destructive excavation is less and less necessary and sites under the surface of the ground can now be visualised. We could make comparison with the rapid developments in medical technology such as the use of endoscopy and laser cutting techniques. Moreover, until comparatively recently, any form of archaeological excavation which 'interfered with the dead' was bitterly opposed in, for example, the Highlands and Islands of Scotland, and this must have been the case in many rural areas. As the availability of information on many subjects at every level increases people's minds are being opened to new possibilities and old prejudices would seem to be in decline.

There are, however, clear instances of ritual death which it is difficult not to envisage as having been of a sacrificial nature, especially in the light of the evidence, classical and otherwise.

Be that as it may, superstition of a very potent nature certainly survived in Europe, virtually up to the present day. The Outer Hebrides of Scotland, to take but one area, possessed a very rich and deeply-rooted corpus of folklore, custom and belief (and some of it undoubtedly must survive in a vestigial form). Yet the inhabitants of these islands are strongly Christian in their belief and practice; but the ways of the ancestors are rooted deep in their collective psyche. This was brilliantly demonstrated by the unique and dedicated collection of folklore and practice as it survived in the nineteenth and early twentieth centuries, by the great scholar Alexander Carmichael. The work, *Carmina Gadelica*, was continued after his death by his grandson James Carmichael Watson, who was tragically killed in the Second World War; the late Professor Angus Matheson of the University of Glasgow edited Volume 5.

Much of the material reveals an archaic paganism which has clearly been adapted to Christian needs. The word *brian* is an ancient word, according to tradition, meaning 'a god'. Thus we learn of, for example, *brian Mícheil*, ('the god Michael') for St Michael. An interesting point here is the fact that the three sons of the great mother-goddess of the Irish divine Tuatha Dé Danann ('people of the goddess Danu') were deities named *Brían, Iuchar* and *Iucharba*. The gods had by no means entirely disappeared from the landscape at whatever time these incantations came into being, and there is a compelling story about a glen in South Uist, Glen Liadail. It was known, certainly, as early as 1716, when it was commented upon by Martin Martin in his important record of his tour to the Hebrides, *A Description of the Western Islands of Scotland*, and the likelihood is that it long antedated this time. In *Carmina Gadelica*, a version of the legend was taken from one John Maclellan (*Iain Bàn*) who was then eighty-two years of age:

Old John Maclellan had a great many old poems and songs got from his father. He had many Ossianic lays, very full and finished, and *containing old words and phrases* not in other versions known to the writer; but these, owing to pressure of work, I was not able to take down.

The story is as follows: Gleann Liadail or Liathadail is a glen in South Uist. no one dared to go into the glen without singing the song to propitiate *daoine beaga* [sic] *a'ghlinne* ('the *little* men of the glen'). (NB: It is clear from this statement and from the poem that the wording should be: *daoine móra a' ghlinne* ('the *great* men of the glen').The only persons who could go were *Clann 'ic Ìosaig* ('the MacIsaacs') ... There are some of this clan in South Uist, who call themselves MacIsaac, and some in North Uist who call themselves MacDonald.

Reilig Ni Ruairidh, ('the burial place of the daughter of Roderick') is in Benmore, near Liadal. It was the custom of the women of Benmore to pour libations of milk on the grave while milking their cows in the neighbourhood. One day, a woman, of less faith than her neighbours, said, in Gaelic: 'I will not pour another drop on the grave of Ni Ruairidh – I see no reason for it.'

Her companions pressed the poor woman not to break the honoured custom, and not refuse the milk, or she would see what would befall herself, or her goods, or her kindred. 'Be that as it will,' she said, 'I will not offer up another drop to the grave of Ni Ruairidh.' Soon after that her son was killed by a leap which he made.The place where the lad had made the leap is called to this day 'the leap of the son of John, son of Alan.'

This site, in South Uist, was known to Martin Martin (1716) by the name of Glen Slyte. It is worth quoting his entry in full:

There is a Valley between two Mountains, on the East-side, called Glen Slyte, which affords good Pasturage.The Natives, who farm it, come thither with their Cattle in the Summer-

Time, and are possessed with a firm Belief that this Valley is
haunted by Spirits, who by the Inhabitants are call'd the great
Men; and that whatsoever Man or Woman enters the Valley,
without making first an entire Resignation of Themselves to
the conduct of the great men, will infallibly go mad. The
Words by which he or she gives up Himself to these Men's
Conduct, are comprehended in three Sentences, wherein the
Glen is twice named; to which they add, that it is inhabited by
these great Men, and that Such as enter depend on their
Protection. I told the Natives that this was a Piece of silly
Credulity as ever was impos'd upon the most ignorant Ages,
and that their imaginary Protectors deserved no such
Invocation. They answered, That there had happen'd a late
Instance of a Woman who went into that Glen without resign-
ing herself to the Conduct of these Men, and immediately
after she became mad; which confirm'd them in their unrea-
sonable Fancy.

The People residing here in Summer, say they sometimes
hear a loud Noise in the Air, like Men speaking. I inquir'd if
their Priest had argu'd against this superstitious Custom. They
told me, he knew better Things, and would not be guilty of
dissuading Men from doing their Duty, which they doubted
not he judg'd this to be; and that they resolv'd to persist in the
Belief of it, until they found better Motives to the contrary,
than had been shew'd them hitherto. The Protestant Minister
hath often endeavour'd to undeceive them, but in vain,
because of an implicit Faith they have in their Priest: and when
the Topics of Persuasion, though never so urgent, come from
one they believe to be a Heretick, there is little Hope of
Success.

These pagan beliefs were clearly so deeply rooted in the minds
of the people, that traces of them have lingered into the twentieth century – and indeed may linger yet where the old traditions
are so valued. I have recounted this tale, which does not in itself

inform us of human sacrifice, but which may ultimately be relevant to an archaeological discovery on the same island.

Pennant tells us that every great family in the Highlands and in the Hebrides had its own Druid who foretold the future and recounted past beliefs to it. Several other later informants convey similar information and when some of the old people have mentioned Druids in the course of telling me a story about some festival such as Beltain, I have noticed that they all use a peculiar tone of voice and speak in a hushed and surreptitious way, almost looking over their shoulders in case they are overheard. There is no doubt at all that ancient beliefs, which were so deeply rooted in the minds of a people whose mode of transmission was essentially oral, were not easily discouraged by priest or minister, and fragments of these may still be collected in the 'field' in the remaining Celtic countries. Their ultimate demise will not be due to ecclesiastical or any other kind of opposition, but to the 'new' distractions offered by television, videos and computer games. The young now rarely show any interest in their native past.

To return to Glen Liadail: we have seen that the gods of this glen were believed to be great in size, a feature of all the stories of deities in the entire Celtic tradition. There is little doubt, too, as Professor Chris Grooms has shown in his excellent book *Cewri Cymru* (1993) that these giants are ultimately the old deities of the land the legends of which are still to some extent remembered, even to this day, in the remoter parts of Wales, as elsewhere by those who have been brought up in such areas.

It is perhaps singular that, on the same island as the haunted Glen Liadail, a discovery of what can only be called 'ritual activity' was made near the north-west point of South Uist (Hornish Point). This consists of a remarkable Iron Age burial. The site was excavated during the 1980s. 'Marine erosion of a low sandcliff had revealed archaeological deposits and structures over a length of fifty metres and standing some fifty centimetres high' (Barber, J. *et al.*, 1989). From our point of view, the most fascinating feature of the excavation was the discovery of a group of four pits. Overlying these was a wheelhouse with associated deposits. One of the radial piers of the wheelhouse partly covered the group of pits. Pits 1, 3 and 4 contained both human and animal bone, pit 2 contained only human bone. The pits had been infilled with sand. The human bones from the four pits were those of a single individual. The skeleton was clearly disarticulated. The teeth suggested that death had occurred at about ten to fourteen years of age, twelve years of age being a reasonable assumption. It is difficult to determine the sex of skeletons of young people, but certain features would seem to indicate that the victim was male. Two of his vertebrae bore deep cuts from a sharp implement.

This remarkable site would certainly suggest ritual, including human and animal sacrifice. It is suggested that the child could have been found, cast up by the sea after drowning. However, Celtic tradition and belief has a long, consistent history; insofar as ritual is traceable in Celtic contexts, especially when supported by the records of writing or reliable folk tradition, there are good reasons for considering these with care. There is a great deal of evidence amongst the Celts at all stages for a superstitious fear of disturbing the places of the dead, taking back from supernatural forces things that have been or may have been offered; and things thrown up by the sea, such as human bodies, were usually returned to that element in the belief that, as the sea had claimed them, they belonged to it. Had this child been cast up in this way, one feels he would either be returned to the sea, or buried near some sanctuary or other sacred place. To go to such elaborate and unpleasant lengths as to prepare four pits to take his remains and to add to these young animals of use to the community, and at an age at which they would not have reached their greatest economic value, would seem to me to signify a complex sacrificial ritual (cf. Brunaux, 1988). Although I am aware that one should not be too hasty in envisaging human sacrifice, there is no doubt whatsoever, as we have seen, that it *did* take place amongst all the Celts, and probably to a considerable extent, if we are to accept the comments of the classical writers, together with the written and oral repertoire of the Celtic world in general. The Outer Hebrides were regarded as more or less uninhabited in the early Irish tradition and were considered to be possessed by demons.

A second site, the wheel-house (i.e. a house built in the shape of a wheel), *A' Cheardach Bheag* ('the Little Smithy') on the Machair of Drimore, South Uist, is situated a short way down the coast from the site we have been discussing. It has many interesting features: there was a complex hearth in the centre of the wheel-house. Running out about 2ft 6ins from this hearth, there was a kerb-like setting consisting of about 20 lower jaw bones of red deer. The head of each jaw was thrust into the ground so that the bone was above and the teeth below, facing downwards. It is, perhaps worth noting that a similar feature was discovered in another South Uist wheel-house, the bones this time being the jaws of pigs, which were particularly sacred to the Celts. The Celts venerated the pig but they also enjoyed eating it and its flesh was the choice food of the feast.

Turning now to Ireland, that enigmatic island with its Gaelic or, as philologists know it, its Q-Celtic, Goidelic, language, its vast corpus of vernacular material, literary and oral, both poetry and prose and its ancient legal documents, many as yet untranslated because of the difficulty of the early Irish language. In this treasure-house of lore and legend, history and pseudo-history, numerous lives of the Irish saints – which are an invaluable source for both pagan and Christian tradition – we possess an astonishing wealth of ancient ceremonial monuments, sacred wells, hill-tops for ritual pilgrimage and peat bogs that have continuously yielded up treasures of great value, some of which may have been offerings to the dark deities, others (and perhaps less likely) lost by those crossing the treacherous terrain perhaps on the so-called 'corduroy roads'. Moreover, many bodies have been found and we may ask 'Was he lost, or was he pushed?' In

other words, was he – or she – a sacrificial victim? At this time
(the Iron Age) 'massive roadways of wood were built across the
bogs, on a scale of construction far greater than anything previously attempted' (Raftery 1994, 65). There were also numerous
great sites which were, until recently, described as hill forts but
the fact that they were defined by impressive earthen ramparts,
having internal ditches, now strongly suggests that they were
ceremonial, rather than defensive sites. Going back to a much
earlier period, great burial sites such as Newgrange, in Co.
Meath and other Neolithic passage graves and ancient burial
mounds are likely to have been revered by the people of Ireland
as places in which the dead ancestors were placed, and these on
occasion became ceremonial centres during the Iron Age.
Moreover, sometimes Iron Age burials were introduced into the
side of such mounds; also skulls, or parts of skulls, for example at
Carrowmore, Co. Sligo, had been inserted into one of the
Neolithic tombs. Rúfus Festus Avienus, who flourished in the
fourth century AD refers to Ireland in a poem as *Insula Sacra* ('the
Sacred Island'). In view of this abundance of impressive archaic
monuments, some of the stones of which were elaborately
carved and decorated, it is not surprising that he should have
regarded Ireland in this light. He may not have been far from the
truth.

There can be little doubt that many ancient standing stones,
decorated or plain, served as cult objects. The *Lía Fáil* at Tara *(11)*,
seat of the kings of Ireland, is an example and there are other
decorated stones throughout the landscape, some of which
would seem not to be in their original position. The badly
damaged, carved standing stone from Killycluggin, Co. Cavan, is
described in the prose *Dindshenchas* as *Crom Cróich*, a king idol
standing on the plain which was called *Magh Slechd* ('the Plain of
Lamentations') near a group of smaller standing stones. He was
believed to have been a tyrannous god who demanded the sacrifice, in his honour, of the first-born of all who who settled in
Ireland. The standing stones were believed to have originally

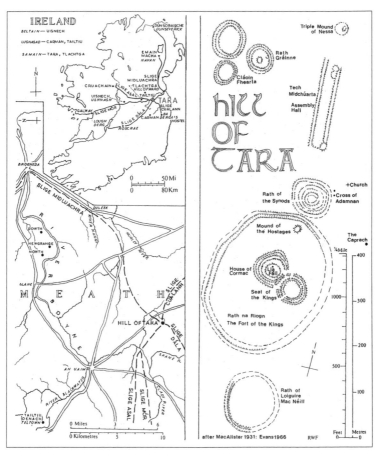

11 Location maps and ground plan of the
Hill of Tara, Co. Meath, Ireland

been placed round the idol. St Patrick, according to tradition, outraged at the heathen excesses of this cult, is alleged to have taken a sledgehammer and attacked the idol with it and so destroyed the power that it had wielded over the superstitious minds of the people.

While doing fieldwork on custom and belief in Co. Cavan with the late T.J. Barron, former headmaster of Bailieboro School, we went to visit the site. It was surprising to find the remains of the carved idol – the lower part of his body, his skirt or long tunic beautifully decorated with spiral carvings – in the very pit into which Patrick had allegedly cast him, his satellite idols in a circle in the wood behind. Mr Barron was puzzled by some aspects of the site before us. Although it was a Sunday afternoon and he knew no one in the neighbourhood, he said: 'I'll just go up to that house there and see what they heard about it. I won't be long.' Some two hours later – a time which passed all too quickly as we were able to study the whole site closely – he reappeared saying: 'Well, he heard a different story about the idol. I asked him where he got it from, and he said from his great-grandmother.' It was a delight to find that their ancient heritage was still a source of fascination to these people, for whom the past had the living quality which had survived down the centuries. Several other important episodes occurred during this particular field trip. Mr Barron had for many years kept close watch over the peat-diggers in his own locality. One day, as he approached the peat banks, he saw a man with a large stick-like object in his hand. He approached him and asked him what he was going to do with it. It was, in fact, an important late Bronze Age/early Iron Age carved figure of some deity. 'Sure,' the man answered, 'I'm going to throw it back into the bog-hole. We're getting dozens of these carved sticks and putting them back. You see, you can't take what's been offered. The other day, one of us got a beautiful bowl, bronze or gold it was, carved and decorated all over.' 'Where is that, then?' asked Mr Barron. 'Oh. we threw it back at once,' he said, 'It would've been ill-luck to have kept it.'

Nevertheless, the school-master managed to retrieve the *Ralaghan* wooden idol, and it is now housed in the National Museum of Ireland. Amongst the other treasures he saved for future generations was the three-faced stone head found on Corleck Hill, Co. Cavan *(plate 19)*, and now likewise in the National Museum; it is sometimes called the Corleck god. Mr Barron, who was a researcher for the Irish Folklore Commission, was told that there had been three passage graves on Corleck Hill, and also an ancient well which was regarded as 'special', although it was probably not a *holy* well. An old woman spoke of two idols with two or three faces having been excavated near the Giant's Grave, but they no longer existed. They do, in fact, exist: the second head was actually janiform, having a human head carved on one side and a ram head conjoined with it on the other. At some stage the two heads had been carefully separated; there must have been some local legend about this. It is interesting to speculate what other treasures the peat-cutters from this area of Co. Cavan must have brought to light. Mr Barron pointed out that in earlier times Corleck Hill must have been isolated by bogs and marsh which surround it on all sides. This, of course would account for the still rich oral traditions that survived in Co. Cavan for so long, many of which were carefully recorded by Mr Barron, who, sadly, died in 1994. He told me that stone heads, such as those we have described above, were widely used in the great calendar festivals (see Chapter 7).

Because such stone heads were clearly surrogate sacrificial heads, and therefore abhorred by the Church, groups of them used to be kept in secret places such as we have seen for the Corleck heads, or buried in some safe spot, often beside a sacred well. They were then uncovered and played their own singular rôle in, for example the Lughnasa gatherings, which are still carried out, in some form or another, in parts of Ireland. Often they must have been set up on some sacred mound. MacNeill, in her brilliant book on the festival of Lughnasa, gives several examples of this motif. One is a story about *Coirpre Crom* and St Ciarán of Clonmacnois preserved in the Book of *Uí Máine*. Coirpre Crom was killed, and his head was placed on a flagstone at the beginning of harvest. The saint recovered the body and the head, banished a demon from the head, joined the two together, and revived the corpse. There is a legend that Crom Dubh was buried for three days with his head alone above ground. These legends together with the Corleck Hill heads already discussed, seem to support the theory that there was a custom of taking a stone head from a nearby sanctuary and placing it on top of a hill for the duration of the Lughnasa festival. As MacNeill (1962, 411 & 426) notes, in early Gaulish iconography, the cavalier god, mounted on a rearing horse, has a great stone head depicted in front of it as if emerging from the ground, or placed on the ground *(12)*, seems to be relevant to the Irish myth and may portray an actual rite

12 Severed head between the feet of the horse of a Rider God; Neschers, Puy-de-Dôme, France

RWF

0 Inches   12   24

0 Centimetres   30   70

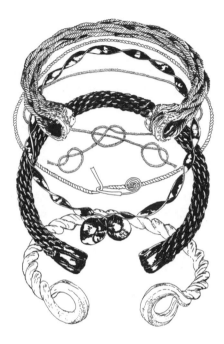

13 Torcs *(from top)*
Needwood, Tara, Tara,
Lindow Moss garotte,
Glascote, Ipswich

(McNeill 1962, 426). The cult of the head is so well-attested, both in the early Celtic world and in later folk survivals, that we cannot do more than glance briefly at it in this context.

To return to sacrifice, although many scholars have tried to deny the practice as a feature of Celtic religion, there can be no doubt whatsoever that it was carried out, and many references to human sacrifice remain in folklore and in folk festival. There is also a great deal of archaeological evidence which is strongly suggestive of this practice, but this of course can often be difficult to prove. One example amongst many of the problems of proof of sacrifice has recently been demonstrated by an enigmatic Iron Age burial discovered above the valley of the river Nene, to the south of Northampton (*Current Archaeology* 159 p 92ff).

A group of circular pits was found within a sub-square enclosure and, while excavating the largest pit, the back of a human skull was uncovered. Further excavation revealed an adult inhumation burial. The skeleton was that of a woman aged between 30 and 40 years, a usual age group for sacrifice, who had apparently been thrown into the side of the pit face down and tightly bound: the arms lay crossed beneath the chest and the legs were flexed, pulled up so far towards the chest that they must have been bound in this position, according to the excavator. This burial ('the Iron Age torc burial'), strongly suggestive of ritual practice, was further distinguished by the discovery of a metal torc of unusual style, which encircled the neck of the victim *(13)*. The most remarkable feature of this ornament was the fact that it had been fashioned in two separate pieces: a detail which to date seems to be unique. Moreover, the metal was basically lead and this in itself is noteworthy. It is a metal not usually associated with adornment such as jewellery, being of considerable weight; and the crude nature of the metal and the trussed position of the body may suggest some form of ritual murder, or of a woman accredited with powers of witchcraft, of some malign influence, or perhaps the Evil Eye (*Current Archaeology*, 159 pp.92-95).

Of great interest is the fact that near to the Iron Age torc burial, a little further down the hill, a small seventh century AD burial ground containing the remains of some 23 individuals was found. They were of all ages, including infants, and five of them had injuries which appeared to result from assault with a blunt instrument rather than accident; all the injuries had healed uneventfully; the population seemed well-nourished and to have had access to good medical care. Of greatest interest, however, was the fact that one of the males had a hypoplastic hamulus (a rare deformity of one of the bones of the wrist), a defect which was shared with the woman from the Iron Age torc burial. Because of its rarity in the the modern population (1.4% of individuals) the shared deformity could well indicate a genetic link between the Iron Age woman and the seventh century man. If this were the case it would demonstrate that the same site had been occupied for almost a millennium.

Another remarkable site, dating to about the mid-first century AD, is a grave in a quarry site at Stanway, near Colchester, which was being excavated in 1996 and is referred to in *Current Archaeology* 153 (pp. 337-342) as 'a burial ground of the native princes ... The latest discovery is one of the subsidiary graves, that of a doctor, buried complete with surgical instruments and his gaming board.' The gaming board, which is dated to about AD 50, had the pieces set up, ready for play, which appears to make it a unique find. Even more impressive was the fact that lying on top of the board was the first medical kit to be recognised as such and revealing that the deceased had been a medical practitioner: a surgeon, as the nature of the tools found strongly suggests. One of the many professional skills of the Druids was the art of medicine and healing. Board games, especially a game similar to chess and called, in Early Irish *Fidchell*; Welsh *Gwyddbwyll* (as in *Fid/gwydd*: wood, wooden; *ciall/pwyll*: wisdom; therefore 'wooden wisdom', were extremely popular in the Celtic world amongst the nobility. The presence of such a gaming board in conjunction with the surgeon's instruments, and the rods and rings possibly for divinatory purposes, would support the excavator's suggestion that the deceased may have been a British Druid. *Fidchell* was only played by those of high rank, such as princes and Druids; divination was one of the functions of the Druids; and Druids were, of course, amongst their many other skills, healers.

Another grave of equally singular and more sinister significance was excavated recently in Ireland, in an Iron Age cemetery of 30 inhumation graves. The graves were situated around the great Neolithic mound of Knowth, in Co. Meath. The grave of most interest in the present context is one which was found to contain a double burial of a dramatic nature. Two adult males lay head to toe in a single pit. Somewhat enigmatically, both had been decapitated. They would appear to have been playing a board game. Glass and bone beads were found, some rings of metal, together with bone dice and other gaming pieces. The radiocarbon date of the burial is 40 BC – AD 100.

Children are frequently represented in burials. These often occur with the remains of adults. This is not surprising when in one of the cremations at Carrowjames, Co. Mayo the remains of an unborn foetus accompanied an adult, believed to be female. When children, ranging from five to nine years of age, accompany adults to the grave, the reason is less clear. In fact, at Carrowjames, children were exclusively buried with adults, with the sole exception of a 6-year-old, whose remains were accompanied by what may have been those of a very small child, perhaps newly born. Double burials such as this are open to interpretation in a number of ways. As Professor Raftery says, the possibility of human sacrifice cannot be ruled out. There is certainly a great deal of evidence for such a practice in other parts of the wider Celtic world. Human remains, of putative Celtic Iron Age date, from two of the Neolithic tombs at Carrowmore, could likewise be thus interpreted. The most striking example, however, is the presumptively Iron Age burial from within the embanked enclosure at the Curragh, Co. Kildare. Buried centrally inside the enclosure lay the skeleton of a woman 'whose strained and awkward position and unnaturally raised skull suggested that she had, in all probability, been buried alive'.

The front cover of the 125th issue of *Current Archaeology* (July/August 1991) presents a somewhat startling picture of a human skull wearing what has obviously been some kind of metal diadem. With the loss of flesh the crown has fallen down over the eye sockets, adding to the dramatic impact of the whole. This impressive object does, in fact, come from a site in Deal, Kent, a housing estate in the process of being constructed. This is no ordinary site, however. It is remarkable in many ways, but by far the most striking feature is the Iron Age burial, to which the said skull belongs. But first, it will be useful to glance at other material revealed at the site, which itself looks so very ordinary in the photograph of the developing estate. It is situated on a low chalk ridge, Mill Hill, just inland from Deal. It soon became clear to the excavators that there had been human activity on the hill

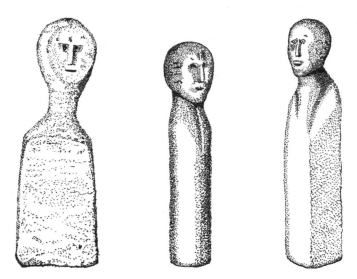

14 Stone figure from shaft, Deal, Kent. Compare two figures from Rochdale, Lancashire, England

for many centuries. There is evidence for a presumptive Bronze Age barrow, of which only a field name remains ('the White Barrow'). The barrow was a focal point down to the Anglo-Saxon period, when two cemeteries were created round it. The Iron Age burial, that of a Celtic nobleman, was not on the site of the original barrow, but its orientation was in that direction. Neolithic pits were found; Late Bronze Age and Early Iron Age finds of pottery suggest settlement in the vicinity. There were also two Iron Age cemeteries and the grave of the Iron Age (Celtic) nobleman, who was the owner of the skull described above. A fascinating aspect of this complex site was a subterranean shrine, at the bottom of a shaft, 3m deep, widening at the bottom, where three or four people could crouch, and where a chalk statue of some deity *(14)* stood in a niche from which it must have fallen when the shaft was infilled in the Roman period. This still remains unique and must throw new light on Celtic religion. In

the early Roman period the site reverted to farming. No more
excavations can be carried out, as the site has entirely vanished
under the housing estate.

Having set the scene for the discovery of the burial to which
the skull belongs, we must look at this in more detail. The grave
was on the north-western corner of the site described above. The
warrior had been buried with sword and shield and the remarkable, decorated bronze headband. There was also a bronze cross-
band running over the top of the skull. This was clearly a crown or
ritual headdress (cf. *plate 3*). The most splendid item was a sword
in a bronze-decorated scabbard. The scabbard had been attached
to the belt by a ring ornamented by pink coral, the finest Iron Age
decoration. The belt itself also had a fitting decorated with pink
coral. A shield, evidenced by its bronze binding, had been placed
on or beside the body. Its shape was totally new for the British
Iron Age, the elongated point at each of its four corners being
composed of a triangular piece of bronze.

This item is perhaps the most important from the cult point of
view, to which we will return. There was also a superbly decorated brooch. This was inlaid with pink coral and another interesting feature of the burial is that, instead of being placed by his
shoulder, as is normal (since brooches were used to fasten the
cloak which was a customary feature of Celtic dress) it was found
down by his legs. The immediate impression conveyed by this
burial is that the deceased held a very high rank in society. I
would suggest that he was a powerful prince, king and/or Druid,
all of whom belonged to the highest echelon of society. No
British Iron Age grave has contained so many fine examples of
Celtic art. These objects date to around the second century BC,
and the excavator comments that nothing could be regarded as
having been imported. Everything was of British manufacture.
One or two of the items are of some significance to early Irish
textual references.

To start with the shield: votive shields of this design have been
found in various places in Britain, including rivers, and Dr Ian

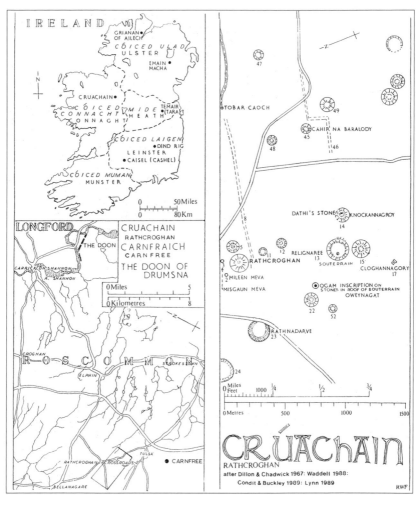

15 Location maps and ground plan of Rath Crúachan,
Co. Roscommon, Ireland

Stead has written a fascinating book in this series (*The Salisbury Hoard*, 1998) which has fine illustrations and the remarkable information that some 24 small bronze votive shields of this kind, together with 46 miniature cauldrons, were found in a pit containing archaeological objects from several early periods. The site is not far from Salisbury.

The great corpus of early Irish literature is rich in stories of decapitations, battles and forays, Druidic ritual and detailed descriptions of the garments and the weapons of the noble warriors. These are of unequal value in terms of identifying archaeological contexts, but it would take an enormous length of time and a good knowledge of the Early Irish language for a comprehensive corpus of such descriptions to be compiled. However, with the above ritual votive shields in mind, I did have a quick look through the longest and finest Old Irish epic, the *Táin Bó Cuailnge* ('the Cattle Raid of Cooley'). The oldest version, Recension I (edited by Cecile O'Rahilly) begins with a description of the mustering of the host. There are various shields in this description, none to match the Deal example, but there is an interesting passage of relevance to Druidic ritual, and in translation this reads: 'So then the four provinces of Ireland were gathered together in *Crúachain Aí (15)*. Their prophets (*fáthi*) and Druids (*ocus a ndruí*) did not permit them to go thence, but kept them for a fortnight, awaiting an auspicious omen.' When the battle is well advanced, the king, Conchobor mac Nessa, King of the Province of Ulster, son of Cathbad the famous Druid, went to meet Fergus. 'He raised against him his shield, the *Ochaín* – all important weapons were given names in early Irish literature – which had *four golden points*, and four coverings of gold'. This is surely a full-sized example, in a literary context, of the miniature shields which are seemingly of a votive nature.

The position of the brooch in the Deal grave is also interesting. In the Irish text *Death Tales of the Ulster Heroes*, we find, in the story of the death of the great warrior Cú Chulainn, the motif of the brooch recurring in the context of death. The hero was resting after long and arduous fighting while his enemies tried for the last time to defeat him. Various omens occurred, foretelling his imminent death. His territory became filled with smoke and flame; all the weapons fell from their racks, and the day of his death drew near. These evil tidings were made known to him and the two women who were present told him to get up from his bed so he leapt up to seize his weapons, flinging his cloak about him, but the brooch which had fastened his cloak fell down and pierced his foot. *This was a forewarning of death to him.* He seized his shield and ordered his charioteer, Loeg, to harness his horse, the *Liath* ('Grey') of Macha, but the horse refused to obey the charioteer. He returned to Cú Chulainn in a state of angry bewilderment. He told Cú Chulainn he must come and speak with the *Liath* himself. However, when Cú Chulainn went to the horse, it turned its *left* side to its master three times, a very bad omen. On the previous night, the war goddess, the *Morrígan*, had broken the hero's chariot, for she did not like him going to the battle; she knew that he would never return to Emain Macha. Then Cú Chulainn reproached his horse, saying that this was not the way he normally treated his master. At that, the loyal beast came to the hero and big, round tears of blood fell on Cú Chulainn's feet. Then Cú Chulainn leapt into the chariot and started it up suddenly. From then on events moved swiftly towards his inevitable death (Cross & Slover 1936, 333-4).

The brooch in the early Celtic world was one of the symbols of status and regarded as of supreme importance. The above examples indicate that when not in its usual place, i.e. in the cloak, but, for example, by the feet of a dead or doomed person, it was a sinister sign. There is another story, belonging this time to the Fenian tradition, which may have relevance in this context. Fionn and his followers come upon the women from the Sídhe Mound. They are standing outside the entrance to the Otherworld mound, weeping. Concerned, Fionn asks them the reason for their distress. One of them answers, saying 'they have lost their brooches and thus cannot get back into the mound of

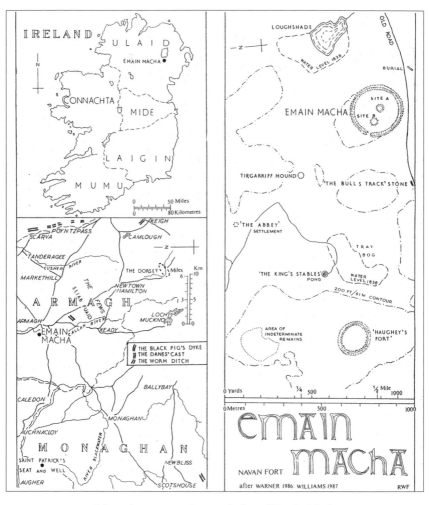

16 Location maps and ground plan of Emain Macha,
Navan Fort, Co. Armagh, Northern Ireland

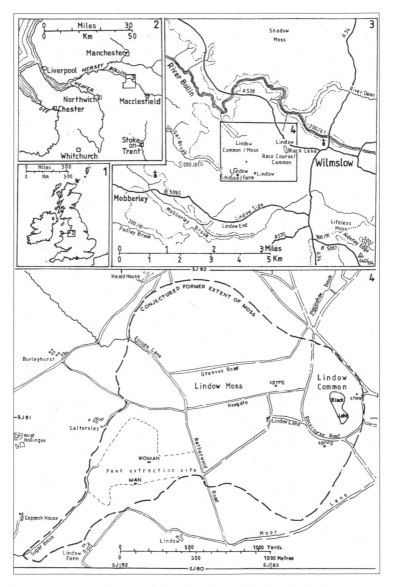

17 Location maps of Lindow Moss, Cheshire, England

Brí Leith.' The brooch would seem to be associated with the Otherworld yet again, and to be essential for re-entrance into the world of the *Sídh* (fairies).

The brooch also occurs in another supernatural context, according to the Irish tradition. It figures in one of the early Irish legends, which describes how the great ritual stronghold of Emain Macha, (Navan Fort) *(16)* had its boundaries marked out by the war goddess, Macha, who used the pin of her brooch to delineate its extent.

Although the remains of human bodies have been found widely throughout the Irish bogs, very few of these – for superstitious or other reasons – have been subjected to the kind of intensive scientific study that was accorded to the bodies found in Lindow Moss, Cheshire, England *(17)*, from August 1984 onwards. There is a certain reluctance on the part of scientists to accept the theory that any or all of these, and indeed other deaths, could have had a ritual import – in spite of factors which would seem to make such a conclusion at least a possibility. The remains, consisting of the head of a female and two badly damaged male bodies, are dated to about the middle of the first century AD, when human sacrifices continued to be offered to some unpredictable deity or deities; prisoners of war and criminals were usually chosen. However, as Caesar, amongst other early authorities wrote (*De Bello Gallico*, VI, 16): innocent victims were unhesitatingly used when the supply of malefactors was exhausted. There is thus strong evidence for human sacrifice from one in high authority (Julius Caesar) who lived contemporaneously with those Celtic tribes to whom he attributes such a zeal for worship and the practice of human sacrifice. Meanwhile, conflicting opinions about bog bodies in general, and the Lindow examples in particular, which may be resolved by future discoveries and research, continue.

As far as Ireland is concerned, I had quite a lot of information about such discoveries in the peat bogs of Co. Cavan, from my colleague the late T.J. Barron. As mentioned earlier, he kept a close eye on the peat-cutters in his area and was aware that parts of human bodies or entire bodies were known to have been uncovered from time to time but they were treated with the respect which was always accorded to the dead and immediately put back. This situation has changed in recent years, with many bog finds being collected: one or two of these are of potential interest but much further study remains to be done.

Human remains have been found in the Scottish bogs, and there may well be finds unreported for reasons of superstition, perhaps, or unwillingness to attract public attention, but many objects of metal have been recovered, and finds of wooden kegs filled with a substance which was identified as butter and thereafter called 'bog butter' are known. Various mundane suggestions have been made about the presence of these wooden kegs in the bogs, for example, to preserve the butter for future use, which seems rather unconvincing; more likely, perhaps, they were propitiatory offerings to the sinister supernatural inhabitants of the dangerous bogs. Offerings were, of course, made into the bogs for the protection of the stock certainly up to the present century, and there were many charms and incantations for the same purpose, which are recorded by the great collector, Alexander Carmichael. It is noteworthy that the goddess/saint Brigit's association with cattle and dairy produce is very much in evidence in this rich repertoire of protective charms and incantations.

There are at least two bogs in Wales which are closely similar in composition to Lindow Moss, which is likewise a raised bog; interestingly, such bogs are normally found in highland regions such as those of Scotland. Like Lindow Moss, Borth Bog (*Cors Fochno*) which still covers a very large tract of land, runs almost to the sea at Borth, on the coast of mid-West Wales. It is widely regarded as an inauspicious and sinister place, and many legends are associated with it. One particular feature near Ynys-las is a so-called bottomless pool, known as *Pwll Du* ('Black Pool'), the guardian of which is a fearsome *gwraig* ('hag'), 7ft tall, who would

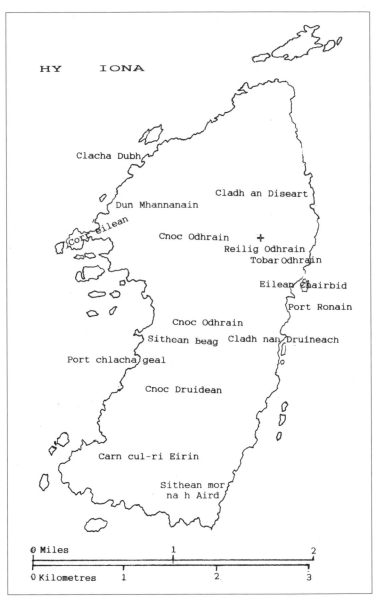

18 Map of Hy, Iona, Strathclyde, Scotland

appear on foggy nights and who traditionally terrified peat-cutters who ventured too near her terrain. One legend tells how those who take peat from anywhere on the bog near the Black Pool are punished by the malevolent guardian, the hag, who follows them to their home and, when an opportunity arises, enters the house and breathes 'germs' and other forms of sickness into the rooms, thereby causing illness in those who dared to steal her peat. The local schoolchildren still sing a song about the hag of Borth Bog and people still experience an uncomfortable sense of the presence of dark forces in the general region of the bog. There seems to be no record of any human remains having been disturbed by peat cutting. Were this so it is very probable that they would be hastily returned to the bog, in the supposition that they were either the remains of some lost person or sacrificial offerings. It is worth noting that Lindow seems to be a British or Welsh word, *Llyn Du* ('black lake'), which is comparable to the *Pwll Du* of Borth Bog.

If we travel some 17 miles south and slightly east from Borth Bog, we come to Tregaron Bog, another large area of bogland, of the same composition as that of Borth. Peats were likewise cut here and I was told of the discovery of a body there some 50 years ago: no further details were forthcoming. Bodies have indeed been found in peat bogs throughout the country, but we cannot conclude, unless there is evidence to the contrary, that all of these, or indeed most of them, were in the nature of ritual murders. Peat bogs are notoriously dangerous places and one must also bear in mind murder – rather than ritual murder, which sacrifice must be – or pure mischance. There must be some kind of evidence to allow us to conclude that sacrifice is a possible explanation. In the case of the Lindow bodies, however, matters are very different, and evidence for sacrifice would seem to be incontestable.

Human sacrifices in peat bogs are well attested in northern Europe, especially in Denmark and sites in southern Sweden and Germany, for example. These are beyond the scope of this present work but we may say that comparison with the remarkable material from the Lindow bodies can be extremely enlightening.

I was collecting folklore in the west of the Island of Skye, and talking to an old man, a native of the island, about the Druids and human sacrifice. The island is staunchly Protestant, and the people tend to become silent and suspicious when any reference to this aspect of the pagan past is made. It is not a subject they will normally agree to discuss. My companion, a renowned *sgeulaiche* or story-teller himself, took quite a different view of things. He was prepared to talk about anything and everything, Druids and human sacrifice included. We were talking in Gaelic and I asked him if he had ever heard anything about St Odhran, who was on the Island of Iona with St Columba at the time of the founding of the monastery. Columba was born in Ireland, *c.*521 and in 563 crossed over to the west of Scotland to the island of Hy (Iona) *(18)*, in order to found a monastery and to Christianise the pagan Picts; the Scots were already Christian. My companion assured me that he had indeed heard of Odhran, and that the saying *'Chaidh úir air súil Odhrain'* ('earth went over the eyes of Odhran') was well known.

The tradition was as follows: when St Columba was building his monastery, he requested that one of the Brothers should volunteer to go under the earth, allegedly to stabilise the building. It fell to Odhran to be the victim and Odhran went into the pit and was covered with earth, hence the saying. But that was not the end of it. According to one tradition, after three days and nights had passed, Columba was overcome with curiosity to know what Odhran had seen during his sojourn beneath the earth, so he ordered him to be disinterred. Apparently, when the earth was removed, the poor man sat up and, in answer to Columba's question about what had happened during the time he was buried, replied to the effect that hell was terrible and that heaven was not all that it was supposed to be and Columba, alarmed by this reply, and fearing that this would weaken the faith of the other monks, quickly had him buried again. The

THE WORKS

Unit 49, St. James Centre
Edinburgh EH1 3SL
Tel No: 0131 557-5091
VAT No: 555 2619 34
Head Office: Midpoint Park
Minworth B76 1RN

Visit Our Website At
www.theworks.gb.com

DATE: 24/09/2007 TIME: 13:27
TILL: 0126   NO: 12650043
CASHIER: Nicky

DESCRIPTION	£
Special Deal Book 3	3.00 C

1 PC. TOTAL	£3.00
CASH	£5.00
Change	£2.00

VAT C 0.00% (£3.00): £0.00

Thank You For Your Custom
Please Call Again

Summer Clearout! Now On!

latter part of this story is, of course 'apocryphal' and such things are always related in an especially solemn, subdued voice.

Foundation sacrifices of one kind or another were common-place and there are still people who practise them in some form or another even today. Archaeology would certainly bear this out for the past in relation to both human and animal sacrifice, and modern folklore often tells how the skull of an animal which has died was placed under the threshold of a house, or beneath the hearth, and sometimes one in the upper corners of the old stone fireplaces. Today, in the Celtic countries and even in regions which were formerly Celtic, in Britain and in Europe, such prac-tices are known to have continued down to the present time. Horse skulls were often so employed.

Learning about traditions such as these from people who have grown up with a knowledge of ancient practices which have been handed down from generation to generation, is a curious, and sometimes startling experience. The oral tradition amongst the Celts was deliberately fostered, as we learn from the classical commentators on the Celts. This custom would seem to have arisen in order that the sacred learning and details of ritual prac-tice should be kept away from the uninitiated. Writing was used for business purposes in Gaul, and Caesar remarks that Greek letters were used for this purpose. He also comments how, when some noble person was being cremated, people would throw letters onto the funeral pyre for him to give to dead relatives and friends in the Otherworld. This tradition of oral learning contin-ues in some small measure down to the present day when story-tellers can recite from memory long and complicated tales and ballads, historical episodes, their own genealogies and many items of custom and belief, some with their roots firmly in the pagan traditions of the Celtic past. We cannot necessarily treat such material today as being strictly historically accurate; but it does serve to illustrate the nature of communication in the distant past and the way in which the whole idea of memorising and reciting events to the next generation operated. There was always a strong sense amongst the Celts of the 'fitness of things', the proper way to perform ritual, the correct person or people to oversee communal activity of this nature, and the ill-effects which would be likely to result from inappropriate behaviour. The Druid or Bard of the earliest Celtic world would, after the official demise of the Druid, have been replaced by his traditional successors, the Fili and Bards, on whose shoulders the mantle of the Druid would eventually fall. The power of the Bard, too, would be enhanced, having as he did, the invincible weapons of satire and magic. Truth was of supreme importance in pre-Christian Celtic societies. As the threefold order of Druid, Bard and prophet or Vatis was, officially at least, replaced by the story-teller, so did the guardianship of the truth become his responsibility and a moral commitment.

Chapter 4

THE SYMBOLIC HEAD

The Druids were deeply concerned with the nature of the Otherworld, the world of the gods and the supernatural, and they used various symbols and symbolic objects with which to describe, indicate and offer reverence to these concepts. One of the most prolific of these was the symbol of the severed head. For the Druids, and thus for the Celts who learnt the secrets of their complex religion from their Druidic teachers, the head was the seat of the soul, the centre of being. It was the supreme example of *pars pro toto*, capable of independent life, speech, movement. It had strong apotropaic powers, warning those whose palaces or dwellings it protected of impending evil. It could provide wondrous entertainment at the feast, on earth or in the realms of the gods. It was capable of imparting fertility to the infertile; of changing sorrow to joy. In its threefold form *(19)* – having three faces or three conjoined heads – it was at its most powerful and formidable. The early Celts, like other contemporaries in Europe, were head-hunters. They cut off the heads of their enemies in battle and tied them to the necks of their horses, bearing them home in triumph. The more severed heads a warrior possessed the greater was his reputation as a hero. And as war was the greatest source of pleasure for the Celtic nobles, and fame their chief aim, an impressive display of severed heads – preserved in oil and herbs, or dried – was of vital importance.

19 Tricephalos, Woodlands, Raphoe, Co. Donegal, Ireland

All the sources of evidence available for a study of the early –
and later – Celts testify to the enduring power of this grim
symbol. The classics make a number of comments on this – to
them – distasteful and barbaric custom; the earliest documentary
material in the vernacular, from Ireland, revels in this theme,
omitting no gory detail but possibly exaggerating the numbers of
trophies taken in any one encounter. Later, the Welsh tradition
provides an impressive picture of the same custom of decapitation. In fact the finest story of all concerns a severed head, the
head of Bendigeidfran, 'Bran the Blessed', one of the Four
Branches *(Pedeir Keinc)* of the Mabinogion, that collection of
delightful tales from medieval Wales. Being later in date than the
Irish material, and composed in a somewhat less violent milieu,
direct references to the Druids *(derwydd, derwyddon*; sometimes
dryw, drywon) are lacking or have been expurgated from most of
the texts. However, their former influence can be clearly
detected in many of the earlier traditions, and the story of Bran's
wondrous severed head and many other motifs show the direct

influence of Druidic thinking and belief. The story of the head of Bran, crowned king of the Island of Britain (*Ynys Prydein*) is, in outline, below — the title, however, refers to the king's sister, *Branwen, Ferch Lyr* ('Branwen Daughter of Llyr'). It may help to understand the magical nature of Bran's head if we appreciate that he was a divinity, not a mortal man and the main characters in the story were probably deities in origin although that is not made clear in the tale. Bran was so huge in size that he could never enter an ordinary dwelling and a special pavilion had to be made for him. The Celtic gods are always depicted as being large and tall in comparison to mortal beings, and this gives some credence to the idea that the numerous giants in Celtic mythology and legend were ancient gods.

The early part of the story is concerned with the courtship of Bran's lovely sister who is described as being *tecaf morwyn yn y byt*, 'the fairest maiden in the world'. Her suitor was the king of Ireland, Matholwch. He crossed from Ireland with 13 fine ships and came ashore at Harddlech, Bran's court. Bran sent his men down to the shore to find out who the men in them were and the reason for their coming. Not only did the king of Ireland seek Branwen's hand in marriage: he wished to unite Britain and Ireland *(ynys y Kedeirn ac Iwerddon)*. Bran son of Llyr was delighted by both these proposals. He sent his messengers to invite the king to land so they might discuss these issues and take counsel. There was a great banquet that night and on the next day, after the matter had been discussed, Bran's sister was given to Matholwch. A time was fixed for him to sleep with her at Aberffraw and the two parties set out for that court, Matholwch and his men in their ships and Bran and his hosts by land. At Aberffraw a great feast was prepared. They put up tents because no house could contain Bran. They sat in their correct order and after eating they began to carouse and to converse. Eventually they went to sleep and Branwen slept with Matholwch that night. Everything was joyous and the liaison had every indication of being a happy and beneficial one to both sides when a tragedy intervened.

Next day the question arose as to where the horses and their grooms should be kept. After some discussion the decision was made. They were then put everywhere suitable as far as the shore. Then one day, Bran's treacherous and sinister brother, Efnisien, the trouble-maker, came to the place where Matholwch's horses had been accommodated, and objected. When he heard from the men with the horses that Matholwch had slept with his sister without his consent he was in a wild rage. He attacked the poor horses and mutilated them mercilessly until they were good for nothing. Matholwch learnt of this terrible outrage and savagery. He was shocked and amazed that such violence had occurred after the beautiful and much-loved girl had been given to him in marriage. His councillors said the only thing for them was to return at once to Ireland. As they went to their ships, Bran learnt for the first time what had happened. Matholwch said he could not understand how he had been so insulted after Branwen had been given to him and he had slept with her. Bran's men tried to explain that the terrible thing that had been done had occurred without the knowledge and certainly without the consent of Bran or his councillors and that they were even more distressed and shocked than was he. Matholwch accepted this but said this could not free him from the grave insult. His men went back to Bran and told him what Matholwch had said. The king replied he must not leave them as an enemy and must be stopped. So he sent three fine warriors after Matholwch to offer him every kind of compensation for his dishonour, including his *gwynebwerth* ('honour-price') consisting of a plate of gold as broad as his face and much else besides. Bran told them to explain what sort of man had destroyed his horses and dishonoured him against Bran's will or knowledge; that it was Bran's brother on his mother's side who had carried out this terrible deed. For this reason it would be difficult for him to put Efnisien to death. Bran asked that the king of Ireland would come face to face with him and he would do anything he wished in order to heal the breach that had come between them. The messengers went to Matholwch and told him all this in a conciliatory manner and he said he would take counsel of his men. It was decided to accept Bran's offer and so they returned to the court in peace. The feast was prepared and they sat together as before and Bran and Matholwch began to converse with each other, but Matholwch was sad and listless. Bran felt it was because he had not offered him a sufficiently generous amount of compensation. He promised, amongst other things, to give Matholwch a cauldron with the power of restoring to life any man who had been slain in battle. Next day he would be alive and fit again in everything, but the power of speech. That could not be restored. The Irish king was delighted by this gift. Next day all the horses that Bran owned that had been broken in were given to him and then they went to where the colts were kept and many of these were bestowed on the wronged Irish king.

That night, after generous reparation had been made to Matholwch, Bran and Matholwch were conversing together and Matholwch asked his host how he had obtained the cauldron that had been made over to him. Bran told him that it had come to him from a man who had been in Ireland; for all he knew the man had found it there. Matholwch asked what the man's name was and Bran replied: 'He was Llasar Llaes Gyfnewid. He came here from Ireland, and his wife with him. They had escaped from the Iron House when it was made white-hot around them.' Bran was surprised that his guest had heard nothing of this story. Matholwch answered saying that he did know of it and would tell Bran all that he had heard. 'One day,' he said, 'I was hunting in Ireland, on top of a mound overlooking a lake called Llyn y Peir ['the Lake of the Cauldron']. And I beheld a big man with yellow-red hair coming from the lake with a cauldron on his back. Moreover he was a monstrous man, big and the evil look of a brigand about him, and a woman following after him, and if *he* was big, twice as big as he was the woman; and they came towards me and greeted me. "Why", said I, "how fares it with you?" "This is how it fares with us, lord," said he, "this woman", said he, "at the end of a month and a fortnight will conceive, and the son who will then be born of that wombful at the end of the month and the fortnight will be a fighting man fully armed." I took them with me to maintain them, and they were with me for a year. For that year I had them with me without grudging; from then on they were a burden to me, and before the end of the fourth month they were of their own part making themselves hated and unwelcome in the land, committing outrage, and molesting and harassing gentles and ladies.

'From then on my people rose against me to bid me part with them, and they gave me the choice, my dominions or them. I referred to the council of my country what should be done concerning them; they would not go of their own free will, nor was there need for them to go against their will, because of their fighting power. And then, in this strait, they decided to make a chamber all of iron. And when the chamber was ready, every smith that was in Ireland was summoned there, each and every possessor of tongs and hammer. And they caused charcoal to be piled as high as the top of the chamber, and they had the woman and her husband and her offspring served with ample meat and drink. And when it was known they were drunk, they began to set fire to the charcoal against the chamber, and to blow the bellows which had been placed around the house with a man to each pair of bellows, and they began to blow the bellows till the house was white-hot around them. Then they held a council there in the middle of the chamber floor. And the huge man waited till the iron wall was white, and by reason of the exceeding great heat he charged the wall with his shoulder and it broke out before him, and his wife after him. And none escaped thence, save him and his wife. And it was then, I suppose, lord,' said Matholwch to Bendigeidfran, 'he came over to thee.' 'Faith', said he, 'it was then he came here and gave me the cauldron.' 'In what manner, lord, didst thou receive them?'. 'I quartered them everywhere in my domain, and they are numerous and prosper everywhere, and fortify whatever place they happen to be in with men and arms, the best that anyone has seen.'

That night they continued to converse as long as they pleased, and sang and caroused. And when they saw that it was more profitable to sleep than to sit longer, to sleep they went. And thus they spent that feast in joy; and when that was ended Matholwch set out for Ireland and Branwen with him. In Ireland there was great joy at their coming. She spent that year in much good fame, and she flourished with honour and with friends. And meantime it came to pass that she grew pregnant, and a son was born to her, Gwern son of Matholwch. He was put out to foster in the very best place for men in Ireland.

The following year however, things changed and rumours against Branwen began to grow, on account of the insult done to her husband by her uncle in Wales. Her husband was mocked for not having avenged those wrongs; and soon the people of his kingdom threatened to rise up against him. Branwen was driven from his bed and made to cook in the kitchens like a common woman. It was forbidden for anyone from Ireland to cross to Wales and any that did so were to be cast into prison. And so it was continued for three years. Branwen took a young starling which came and sat on her kneading trough and she taught it to speak and described Bran to the bird so that it would know him. She wrote a letter telling him everything, and how she was shamed and when it was ready she sent it off with the letter tied underneath its wings. The wise little bird reached Wales and found Bran where he was holding an assembly. It came to rest on his shoulder and ruffled up its feathers so that Bran would see the letter from his sister. The letter was read by Bran and he was sorely grieved at his sister's plight. He dispatched messengers to every quarter of the Island of Britain. He then summoned all the fighting men of the one hundred and fifty four districts and he told them of Branwen's dreadful suffering.

They decided to set out for Ireland as soon as possible. Bendigeidfran and the huge host set sail for Ireland while Bran waded across as he was too large to fit into a ship. He carried all the minstrels with their stringed instruments on his own back and so they came to Ireland. Matholwch's swineherds were on the shore with their pigs, and when they saw the great fleet of ships approaching the land they rushed to tell Matholwch. They told him that they had seen a great forest out to sea where no trees had ever been before. 'Strange' said the king 'could you see anything else?' They replied that they could see 'a great mountain close to the forest, and it was moving, and there was a lake on either side of the lofty ridge of the mountain and everything was moving towards them'. 'Why,' said Matholwch 'no one except Branwen will know anything of that; go and ask her.' Messengers were sent to his wife. 'Lady' said they, 'what do you think that can be?' 'It is the fighting men of *Ynys y Kedyrn* ('the Island of the Mighty') on their way across having heard of my ill-treatment and humiliation.' Finally they asked her, 'What is the high ridge, and the lake on either side of the ridge?' 'He,' she said, looking towards this island; 'he is angered. The two lakes on either side of the ridge are his two eyes, one on each side of his nose.' This description of the great, divine king coming like a giant striding angrily through the deep waters, and carrying his minstrels on his back conveys a marvellous impression of his power and his magic.

All the warriors of Ireland were hastily called upon to take counsel with Matholwch. It was decided to break down the bridge over the *Llinon* (the Liffey) so that none could cross it. Bran landed with his fleet near the bank of the river. His men told him that it was a peculiarity of the river – which had lode-stones at the bottom of it – that no one could go through it, nor was there a bridge. Bran then, in his fury, said that he himself would be the bridge. He placed himself across the river and hurdles were placed upon him and all his warriors were able to cross over. Messengers came to greet him and bring messages from Matholwch. Bran would not have this at all and sent his men back to Matholwch for a different answer. The men told this to Matholwch. The king asked for advice. 'Build a house in his honour' they said, 'for he has never been able to live in a house.

Let Bran and the men of Ynys y Kedyrn live in one half of the house, and do you and your warriors live in the other half. Give over the kingship to him and pay him homage.' They told Matholwch that Bran would be delighted at having a house large enough to contain him and his retinue and as a result he would make peace with him. The messengers came to Bran and after taking counsel, he decided to accept Matholwch's offer; this was all because of Branwen who advised this, because she feared that the whole land would be laid waste otherwise. Matholwch proposed to give the kingship of Ireland to Gwern, Bran's sister's son but Bran refused this. He accepted the offer to build a house large enough to contain him and his retinue. Peace was made and the house was built. But the Irish planned to destroy Bran. There was a great feast in the house and the kingship was given to Gwern. The child went to everyone, and all loved him. But Efnisien seized him and threw him into the fire. Chaos ensued, fighting broke out and nearly everyone was killed. Bran was mortally wounded. The cauldron of regeneration *(peir dadeni)* was placed on a fire but Efnisien destroyed it and so redeemed his evil. Only seven men escaped, taking Branwen with them, and made to return to Wales. Bran told his companions to cut off his head and take it to the Island of Britain.

The seven men, taking Bran's head with them, set out for Harddlech in Merionethshire. There they sat down and began to eat and drink; and three birds came to them and began to sing a particular song. All the songs that they had ever heard seemed dreary to them in comparison with the singing of the birds. In order to see them they had to look far out over the waters; yet the music was as close to them as if it had been in the same room. They remained there feasting for seven years and all the while Rhiannon's three birds entertained them with magical Otherworld music such as they had never before heard. And although their singing sounded close to, they had to gaze far out to sea before they could make out the shapes of the goddess' wondrous birds.

At the end of the seven years they had to set their faces towards *Gwales* (Grassholm Island) in *Penfro* (Pembrokeshire). There they found that a splendid, royal palace was prepared for them which looked out over the sea. There were two open doors. A third door was closed, the door looking out towards Cornwall. 'That' said Manawyddan, 'is the door we must not open'. That night there were provisions of every kind laid out before them; and they were filled with gladness. And of all the sorrows and suffering and grief that they had seen with their own eyes, and that they themselves had endured, they had no memory of these or of any sorrow in the world. And in this manner fourscore years slipped by, and they could not remember a time when things had been different for them. The years did not burden them nor could any one of them tell from the appearance of the others that so great a length of time had passed since they came there. And Bran's head was no more troublesome to them than it had been when he was alive. 'And because of those fourscore years it was called the Assembly of the Wondrous Head' (*ach o achaws y pedwarugeint mlyned hynny y gelwit Ysbydawt Urdaul Benn*). But one day a thought came into Heilyn son of Gwyn's head 'Shame on my beard' *(Meuyl ar uy maryf i)*, said he, 'if I do not open the door to know if that is true which is said concerning it.' So he opened the door that looked out over Cornwall and even as he looked they immediately became conscious of every loss and sorrow they had endured in the past and of all the kinsmen and friends they had lost and they remembered all the evil that had befallen them as if it had only just happened. And above all else, the death of their lord, Bran. From then on they had no peace; they must take the head and set out for London. They eventually arrived, and buried the head in the White Mount *(Gwynfryn)*. When the head was buried it was one of the Three Happy Concealments *(trydyd matcud)* and when it was unearthed was one of the Three Unhappy Disclosures *(trydyd anuat datcud)*. As long as the head remained concealed in the earth no pestilence would ever come across the sea to Ynys Prydein. Its removal from its burial place

∴ OENAICH
- Ancient Irish Assembly Site

coíced
Provinces of
Early Ireland

ULAID
ULSTER

Emain
Macha

CONNACHT
CONNAUGHT

Cruachan
Rath Croghan

MIDHE
MEATH
Tlachtga
Uisneach

Tailtiu

Tara

Carman

LAIGIN
LEINSTER

MUMU
MUNSTER

0 Miles   60

0 Kilometres   100

RWF

20 Coíced, the provinces of Early Ireland,
and Oenaich, ancient Irish Assembly Sites

would let loose all manner of evils on the country. This magnificent tale, the Second Branch of the Mabinogi, ends on a doleful note. In Ireland the only people left alive after the battle were five pregnant women. They were in a cave in wild countryside. Each bore a son at the same time and from these sons the five divisions (coíced) *(20)* of Ireland originated.

In this medieval Welsh story, its sophisticated language and elegance of composition serve to obscure the truly primitive elements that lie just below the surface of its literary expertise. Told in translation it is indisputably powerful; read in the rich and evocative Welsh its powers and pathos are immeasurably increased. The leading characters, with all their potential of wealth, influence and beauty, are doomed from the very start. The story-teller artfully conceals this by creating an idyllic background which seemingly sets the scene for both an ideal political arrangement, and for a joyous personal future for the pure and beautiful Branwen, 'White Raven', and the king of Ireland, Matholwch. The element *math* can mean 'good' or 'bear'. In the mediaeval Welsh Triads the king of Ireland is called *Matholwch Wyddel* ('the Irishman'). He, too, is a mythological or legendary figure. It is also an example of the mythological motif of the sacred severed head. When the head was buried in London, its supernatural powers were to survive. Its purpose changed from delightful companion to evil-averting talisman. There it remained and there was no invasion of the land while it remained in its place of concealment. Tradition has it that it was Arthur who had it unearthed and removed for he would not accept that anyone or anything could protect the Island of the Mighty except himself.

There is another possible site for the interment of the divine head which is very persuasive. Some scholars have felt that London was an unlikely place for it to guard the country. An alternative site might well be Brancaster in Norfolk. In Old British this would be Branodunon, 'Bran's Fort'. Situated close to the sea, in Icenian territory, it would command an excellent view over the coast and the sea across which invasions from the continent would come. It is barely ten miles from Snettisham, the site where a magnificent hoard of priceless Celtic torcs was recovered, a rich terrain in which items of Celtic metalwork and coinage are constantly being recovered, by excavation, or the use of metal detectors. That is a second possibility. However, the traditional view that the White Mount was near St Paul's Cathedral has not been rejected.

Many human skulls have been found in the River Thames and its tributaries along with rich caches of valuable early Celtic metalwork. Moreover, Bran means 'Raven' and there is the legend of the ravens which are still kept in the Tower of London. How old this tradition may be is difficult to determine. Druids are not mentioned in this story with all its traces of an older Celtic world, nor would we expect them to be. The Romans were no more tolerant of Druidism in Britain than were they in Gaul, although no doubt the people themselves kept its memory alive, as did the poets through their ancient craft of word-magic. They would certainly have still been present to some extent in Ireland, and their former influence and fame lingered in the folk memories and household tales throughout the British Isles. Boudica, the great Icenian queen, herself was a Druidess or priestess. The ancient laws, once their Druidic compilers had been replaced by Christianised kings and secular bodies, would have survived in the oral tradition to some extent, but the new rules would have been accepted, nominally at least, after the coming of the Saxon law-makers.

Ine, king of Wessex, for example, was married to a British princess who no doubt wielded some influence in favour of her own background.

The tale of Branwen Ferch Lyr is a masterpiece of literary composition. The characters are portrayed with consummate skill and realism while the action moves from the idyllic beginning to an ever more inevitable horror and hopelessness as disaster follows on disaster and the early hopes of a happy marriage between the

king's sister and the king of Ireland, resulting in the union of two
great kingdoms are blighted. The character of the jealous half-
brother, Efnisien, is portrayed in strong contrast to his 'good'
brother, Nisien, who plays a minor rôle in the story. One of the
most interesting motifs is that of the magical cauldron of regeneration, its arrival in Ireland with the grotesque huge and ill-
favoured couple, their escape from the deadly iron house, a motif
known from several other tales, Irish, and as far afield as India,
which is recounted with a consummate skill in which the tension
mounts as the heat is increased by the use of bellows by the Irish
outside. As the walls become white-hot and escape seems impossible, the mighty monstrous man puts his gigantic shoulder to the
wall and it gives way under his huge weight. As we saw, the couple
escape, the man taking his cauldron with him and the child that
the woman was carrying in her womb when they arrived. Where
they went to after that was not known until Bran was able to tell
the king of Ireland that they had come to him. In some ways the
story is very reminiscent of the Gaelic tradition of the Glenlyon
Hag *(cailleach)* and her husband, the *bodach* ('old man').

One point that may be mentioned here is the fact that when
the great man with the cauldron came to Bran, he gave the
magical vessel to him as a gift. As we saw, he and his gigantic wife

21 Shrine, Glen Lyon, Perthshire, Scotland

bred and they and all their offspring were good retainers and fighting men and he was well-pleased with them. In the Gaelic story (for full details of which see Chapter 9 below) only one child, a girl, is represented. But when I visited the little 'shrine' *(21)* with the shepherd, he showed me several smaller stones which lay on the floor of the dwelling and were believed to have been offspring of the larger stones. There is a strange superstition to the effect that stones do breed and increase. A perhaps relevant belief occurs in the Irish text, *The Ten Signs of the Doom*. The warning that it is nigh will be when all the stones begin to speak. Stones, particular and in general, have always been revered by the Celts.

The continuing significance of decapitation in medieval Wales

Anyone who is at all familiar with British history will be aware that one of the most turbulent regions for many centuries was the terrain known as the Marches. This wide stretch of territory on either side of the Welsh-English borders had always been renowned in history for its restless and resentful attitude to the authority of the English Monarchy, against which it periodically rebelled. This was particularly the case during the High Middle Ages, that is, in the twelfth and thirteenth centuries when revolt on the part of the Welsh and ruthless suppression on the part of the English was the cause of a great deal of bloodshed, violence and frequent decapitation of the defeated by the victors – a practice which can be traced directly back to the comments of the classical writers regarding this custom, as early as the late centuries BC. Tradition tends to linger long in the conservative Celtic consciousness and there are some remarkable examples of this in the Marcherlands, which include some of the most peaceful and idyllic scenery in the British Isles.

One point of particular interest is the difference in significance that decapitation had for both Welsh and English protagonists.

For the Welsh, even at this late period of history, decapitation was a natural and instinctive feature of warfare. The Welsh tended to take the heads of any defeated English enemies and display them, as had their battle-mad forebears and therefore it was a justifiable, rather than a barbaric act. For the English, however, it was essentially different. It was part of their culture to take the heads of their defeated adversaries and display them in some prominent place, often sending them to London. They also did many gruesome things with the bodies, disembowelling them, frequently quartering them and displaying them as a warning to other malefactors. In his *Description of Wales*, written *c*.AD 1132 (Thorpe 1978), Gerald the Welshman (Giraldus Cambrensis) compares the mercenary soldiers from France with the hardy and experienced Marcher soldiers; he notes that, for the French 'the army is an honourable profession, but for us it is a matter of dire necessity', and again, '*they* take prisoners, *we* cut off their heads; *they* ransom their captives, but *we* massacre them.'

We seem once again to have hardly progressed from the attitude of the early Celts when we consider the following anecdote: on 14 June, 1233, the exchequer was instructed to pay Richard de Muneton and his troops 57 shillings for the heads of Welshmen. Seemingly, a substantial group of Welsh raiders, bent on attacking the wealthy manor house of Stratton, perhaps, or the prospect of chancing upon merchants coming along the ancient road through the valley, had crossed the border when they were intercepted by Richard de Muneton, in command of a local defence force. In the ensuing encounter, 57 of the Welshmen were killed. The fact that they were decapitated and the heads handed over to the government which then paid a reward for them and gave Richard a position in government, reveals that the English government was in favour of decapitation against the *Welsh*, for whom it was merely a cultural continuum. This rewarding of troops by cash for heads appears to be the only recorded example of such a practice but there *is* other evidence to demonstrate that the English decapitated their Welsh foes.

Some two years previously, in 1231, after the troops stationed at Montgomery Castle had attacked and defeated the Welsh, the captives were brought to the custodian of the castle, who had them decapitated and their heads were presented to the king. It must be noted that both of these accounts are derived from English sources. The victims' names do not appear to have been recorded, but their numbers would have been obvious from the tally of heads.

Decapitation existed among the medieval Welsh as it did amongst the other Celtic peoples but for them it was an indigenous custom with very different religious and cultural connotations. For the early Celts, the head acted as *pars pro toto*, the symbol, not only of life itself, but of immortality and the soul. It also was the emblem of the victorious warrior who treated the head of the enemy he had decapitated with all the respect that was due to a defeated but worthy enemy; but the treacherous decapitation of that enemy would do nothing to enhance the reputation of the victor, for it would be a breach of the Druidic maxim of 'fair play'.

The cult of the human head did not die out with the official end of paganism; on the contrary, it not only avoided the encroachments of the Christian ethos but survived, and was adopted into early Irish and Welsh hagiographies as the popular motif of the decapitated saint whose head, upon touching the ground, causes a healing spring to well up. The head is frequently reunited with the body by the good offices of another saint. It is a motif which is still very much alive in surviving Celtic folklore, as is the strong belief in the healing power of water from a special spring, when drunk from a venerated cranium in the time-honoured ritual manner. All such heads which were believed to be imbued with special powers, had their own guardians who knew the cult legend and the right ritual.

There are many stories extant about head-taking and displaying. The medieval Welsh story entitled *Gereint son of Erbin* describes a scene which imparts a grim warning to any hero bold enough to approach a magical hedge of mist within which were 'enchanted games'; 'and each and every man that has gone thither has never come back' (G. and T. Jones). The story continues: 'And the court of earl Ywein is there, and he permits no one to lodge in the town save those who come to him at his court.' After feasting Gereint and the guests get ready to go to the games, which are clearly of a sinister character. They come to the magical hedge 'and not lower was the hedge they could see than the highest point they could see in the sky. And on every stake they could see in the hedge there was a man's head, save for two stakes; and many indeed were the stakes in the hedge and throughout it.' This grim image of the trophy-heads and the two empty stakes, obviously waiting to be occupied, is sufficiently compelling and chilling to satisfy even the most ardent of the early Irish head-hunters; and it is also paralleled by the Welsh poet Taliesin's boastful verse:

> I have broken a hundred forts (*Neu vi a Tories cant Kaer*),
> I have killed a hundred seneschals (*Neu vi aledeis cant maer*),
> I have given a hundred garments (*Neu vi arodeis cant llen*),
> I have cut off a hundred heads (*Ni vi aledeis cant pen*).

The poet, Taliesin, was composing his heroic poems in the sixth century. It was a dark and troubled time for Britain *(22)*, but still the old boastful Celtic spirit sang out, recounting deeds and encounters more worthy of the Iron Age than the Dark Ages, typified by residual paganism, struggling Christianity in the north and west of Britain, and beset on the east by the pagan intruders, the Teutons whom Christianity had not as yet touched. It was this period that Gildas reviled so bitterly as he chanced upon rotting and hideous heathen idols for whom he had nothing but scorn and distaste. The chieftains of western Britain did not fare much better, Gildas regarding them as untrustworthy scoundrels. The title of Taliesin's poem is *Marwnat Uthyr Pendragon* 'The Death of Uthyr Pendragon' who was, according

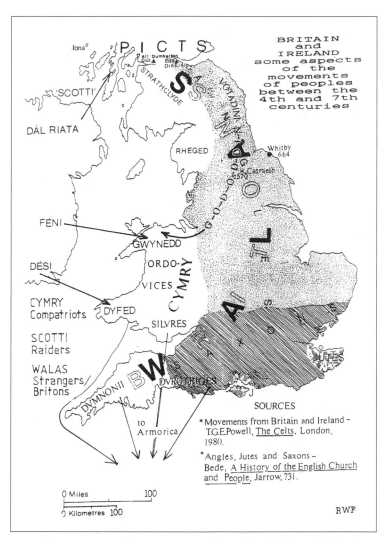

BRITAIN
and
IRELAND
some aspects
of the
movements
of peoples
between the
4th and 7th
centuries

Iona°

P I C T S

'SCOTTI'

DÁL RIATA

Alt Dumbarton
Clút Edin
Din Eidin

STRATH CLYDE

RHEGED

Whitby
664

Catraeth
c570

VOTADINI-GODODDIN

FÉNI

GWYNEDD

DÉSI

ORDO-

VICES

CYMRY

CYMRY
Compatriots

DYFED

SILVRES

SCOTTI
Raiders

WALAS
Strangers/
Britons

DVMNONII

B W

DVROTRIGES

JUTES

to
Armorica

SOURCES

*Movements from Britain and Ireland –
T.G.F.Powell, <u>The Celts</u>, London,
1980.

*Angles, Jutes and Saxons –
Bede, <u>A History of the English Church</u>
<u>and People</u>, Jarrow, 731.

0 Miles   100

0 Kilometres 100

RWF

22 Some aspects of the movements of people in Britain and Ireland
between the fourth and seventh centuries AD

to the tradition, the father of Arthur. One hundred heads is no mean tally.

Even after the Second World War a great deal of folklore and ancient fragments of custom and belief including Druidic lore was still current in Ireland, the Scottish Highlands, Brittany, Man, and in Wales. While collecting stories and sayings in the Scottish Highlands and Islands, where the Gaelic language was still in daily use, I came upon several traditions of a patently archaic character, which still involved a certain amount of ritual. The first and perhaps the most remarkable of these concerned an object much-used by the Druids themselves – a severed head or skull, or a part of a skull. The site was a remote glen in the wild hills of Torridon in wester Ross in the Highlands of Scotland. At some time in the past (perhaps 200 years ago), a human skull was found, seemingly that of a suicide which had come up through the ground outside the churchyard – suicides were not buried within the sacred precincts. The elders recognised it as a means for curing epilepsy and that has been its purpose ever since. The cure is regarded as infallible and is known throughout the Highlands and Islands. There is a special spring which rises on the wild hillside above the township. Its waters are regarded as having their own qualities of purity and healing; the skull is kept close to this spring in a stone box or cist. Persons suffering from *tinneas tuiteamach* (Falling Sickness, i.e. epilepsy) are still given a drink of the water out of the skull (Irish and Scottish Gaelic *cloigeann, blaosc*). People come from all over the Highland and Island regions of Scotland, and even from further afield to be cured of this distressing affliction. A special ritual is an essential part of the healing process.

In the 1960s I visited Torridon, hoping to learn something further about this extraordinary practice which could more properly belong to the Iron Age than to the twentieth century. The guardian of the skull – whose family has held that position since it was first found lying on the ground – was prepared to tell me about the cure, but unwilling to take me to the site. 'They

believe' he said in a solemn voice, 'that if the well is visited for
any other purpose than healing, its powers will weaken'. Feeling
disappointed I then prepared to take my leave of him. 'Be here at
ten o'clock tonight', he said, 'and I will take you there. We must
go up after the last ray of sun has left that hill; and we must be
down before the first light of dawn gleams in the east.' I must
confess to a twinge of trepidation, but excitement at the prospect
of seeing the healing spring with the guardian soon removed any
apprehension. I duly returned to the guardian's home and found
him ready and waiting for me. During our ascent of the dark hill
– he knew every minute feature of it – he told me a great deal
about the ritual involved in the ancient skull-healing rite.
Originally, both the ascent and the descent were to be carried
out in silence. Once the spring of sweet, pure water was reached,
he would go to a nearby place and take the skull from its stone
container. Then, in the name of the Trinity, he would dip the
cup-shaped cranium into the well and give the patient water to
drink from it three times. The well was also circumambulated
three times in the name of the Trinity. The skull had first been
replaced in its cist. 'Then,' he said, 'I put the prohibitions
(*geasaichean*) on the patient.' I was particularly interested to know
about these tabus. At first he refused to describe them to me, but
finally did so, on the understanding that I would never divulge
them to anyone. They were, of course, fascinating, and clearly
very archaic, but I have kept, and will keep, my promise of silence
to him. 'Finally,' he said, 'we descend the hill in total silence.
When we reach level ground again, the cure is complete.' His
healing powers were renowned, not only in the Scottish
Highlands, but in other regions and countries where his cures
had become known. Here, I felt the 'Guardian' was taking over
directly from the Druid, with his marvellous powers of healing,
and only the inclusion of the name of the Trinity in the ritual
differentiated the rite from that carried on down countless
centuries by the ancient Druidic tripartite order. When I had
thanked him and drunk tea in his house, I felt as if I had truly

been carried far back in time to an older Celtic society and a religion that was part of the daily life of the people.

There are other examples of the use of the human skull in contemporary – or near-contemporary – contexts. Another skull, used to cure this same disease of *tinneas tuiteamach*, 'epilepsy', was kept in a churchyard in the island of Lewis in the Outer Hebrides, and was dug up for the cure of this disease. This was done in secret as the Church was very suspicious of such 'heathenish practices'. In Wales, *Penglog Teilo* (Teilo's Skull) is still preserved in Llandeilo, Llwydiarth, Pembrokeshire, and beside it is St Teilo's Well, which is a strong spring rising up within a short distance of the ruined church of Llandeilo. Close by is a farmhouse at which the skull is and has been kept 'from time immemorial'. It is used for drinking the water from St Teilo's Well, which has a wide reputation as a healing well, and people come long distances to visit it, just as they travel from afar to the well at Torridon, Ross-shire.

The rituals associated with St Teilo's Skull were as follows: the skull had to be dipped in the well, filled with water and handed to the hereditary Guardian. The tradition as to how the skull got there is interesting: St Teilo died *c.*566. When I visited the well a few years ago, it was called *Ffynnon yr Ychen*. The skull was brought to me from the farm-house and I held it while legends about it were recounted by the farmer and his wife. There is a stream called Nant-y-Benglog (Stream of the Skull), which is, or was, on the Nanteos Estate near Aberystwyth, Ceredigion. Beside it is a field which was known locally as Maes-y-Clefyd (the Field of Sickness). There does not seem to be any extant tradition about this skull, but it is not improbable that it was, like the Torridon Skull, kept in the field and used in some curative process. Holy wells, which may or may not have been accredited with special powers, abound in Wales, but seemingly St Teilo's in Pembrokeshire was the most widely renowned of these.

The severed human head possessed many powers according to ancient belief, recorded by the classics, and attested by the earliest insular records and later tradition. Many wells, springs and lakes are associated with severed heads throughout the Highlands of Scotland and some interesting legends about them are still current.

The head was truly a symbol of the religion of the early Celts, one which has remained long after the Druids who were in charge of the Celtic religious practices ceased to wield supreme power in society, kept alive by the love and respect that the Celts have always accorded to the old ways and the beliefs of their ancestors.

Chapter 5

THE VERNACULAR LITERATURES

Our knowledge of the Gaulish Druids comes from the classical commentaries, the 'outsiders'. The evidence for the Irish Druids is thus more reliable, coming from direct testimony. Naturally, the Irish writers were not willing to give to the uninitiated a systematic account of the Druidic system. They simply incorporated into their literary writings the doings and sayings of the Druids. The available information from this source is naturally scattered and fragmentary, but it does have a great value. O'Curry (1878, 18 n.38) comments that there are 'vast numbers of allusions to the Druids in the older MSS which it would be quite impossible to unfold at full length...'. The editing of many new texts since he wrote that has of course further increased our knowledge. Stress is laid on Druidic powers of divination, prophecy and magic. These preternatural powers are ascribed to the Druids in *Lebor Gabála* (Book of Invasions) and *Táin Bó Cúailnge* ('The Cattle Raid of Cooley') as in the early Christian chronicles. 'The same emphasis prevails throughout the ancient writings.' There is mention of the straw or grass wisp which when thrown in the face rendered the victim insane; power of protecting an army from defeat by ringing it round with magical fire; showers of fire the Druids had the power to 'call down'. They also made predictions from the clouds, from rods of yew inscribed with Ogam letters, from dreams, from their knowledge of lucky or unlucky days (*vide* Coligny Calendar).

The Druids persisted as a recognisable body during the first centuries of of the Christian era in Ireland. It is noteworthy that during this period they are represented as diviners and magicians.

St Brigit and the Druid

Druids figure prominently in the early life of St Brigit. On one occasion her father, Dubthach, was driving in his chariot with his bondmaid, Broicsech, who was to be the mother of Brigit. They passed the house of a certain Druid, Mathgen, who prophesied that the bondmaid would give birth to a child of great renown. Because of the jealousy of his wife Dubthach sold the bondmaid to a poet who then sold her to a Druid of Tirconnell. This Druid made a great feast to which he invited the king of Conaill whose wife was expecting a child. The Druid foretold that 'the child which should be born at sunrise tomorrow and neither within the house nor without would "outdo" every child in Ireland.' That night the queen gave birth to a dead child. At sunrise the bondmaid bore a child with one foot inside the house and the other outside it. This child was then brought into the presence of the queen's child who was restored to life. The Druid travelled with the bondmaid and her baby into Connacht when, in a dream, he saw 'three clerics in shining garments, who poured oil on the girl's head and thus completed the order of baptism in the usual manner, calling the child Brigit. When she was a grown girl the Druid and his wife went one day to the dairy where their daughter was helping her mother and demanded to have a great hamper, 18 hands high to be filled with butter. The girl had only the making of one churning and a half but, at her prayer, the butter increased so that 'if the hampers of the men of Munster had been given to her she would have filled them all.' Whereupon the Druid freed Brigit's mother, presented to Brigit the butter and the cows, which she gave to the poor and needy, received baptism and remained until his death in Brigit's company. It would seem that stress is laid on the *magical* qualities of the Irish Druids simply because the texts come from within the Irish tradition – the Celts, not through classical or alien eyes, but through native eyes.

It is clear however, that the Irish Druids were not mere magicians. Like the Gaulish Druids, they constituted the learned class of society. But the seat of Druidic learning for Gaulish and insular Druids alike is alleged to have been Britain (Tacitus and Pliny and early Irish texts). In pagan times the Druids were the exclusive possessors of whatever learning was then current. They combined in themselves all the learned professions; they were not only Druids, but judges, prophets, historians, poets, and even physicians. Hyde gives much the same account of the Druids, though with reservations. 'Although Irish literature is full of allusions to the Druids, it is extremely difficult to know with any exactness what they were... They are frequently mentioned in Irish literature as ambassadors, spokesmen, teachers and tutors. Kings were sometimes Druids, so were poets. It is a word that seems to have been, perhaps from the first, used with great laxity and great latitude.' Whatever the truth of this complex order in Ireland may be, the Druids were certainly teachers. Cathbad the Ulster Druid taught many pupils; apart from a variety of other skills and knowledge they learned from him the auspicious days and seasons. Another example dates to early Christian times. In the Tripartite Life of Patrick, we learn that one of the daughters of the king, Loegaire, was tutored by two brothers who were Druids. The Druids were concerned with the gods and with the material world and with origins.

The Book of Invasions

The Book of Invasions is an ancient chronicle purporting to give the origins of the Irish people, and known as *Lebor Gabála Érenn* ('the Book of the Conquest of Ireland). Large fragments of this are found in the Book of Leinster, the Book of Lecan and the Book of

Ballymote. About 1630 a version of it was compiled at the monastery of Lisgoole in Co. Fermanagh by the Franciscan scholar, Brother Michael O'Clery and his helpers. They drew on ancient books, now lost, most of which were written in the twelfth century AD and containing much archaic material and traditions. The Book of Invasions is in both verse and prose; the verses clearly had a mnemonic function, i.e. they were a summary, in verse, of the facts contained in the prose passages. This chronicle was widely known from the Middle Ages on. It was relied upon by the annalists to provide the beginnings of Irish history. *Lebor Gabála* confidently summarises the history of the world from the time of Adam and Eve and follows this with a list of the various 'races' which conquered and settled in Ireland.

Some 300 years after the deluge, a certain Parthalón and his people came to Ireland from Greece. Three centuries later, Nemid came with his sons from Scythia. Soon after, they were troubled by the Fomorians, a race of pirates. There was a huge battle and both sides were almost destroyed. However, three of the Nemidian leaders escaped. One went to northern Europe, one to Greece, and the third, Britan Mael, went to the island of Anglesey. The descendants of the first two, Beothach and Simeon Breac, eventually returned to Ireland. Simeon's descendants were the Firbolgs and Beothach's the Tuatha Dé Danann. The Tuatha Dé established themselves as masters of most of the country at the great battle of Moytura, near Cong, in Co. Mayo. The last colonisation was by the sons of Miledh, who were said to have come from Spain *c.*1,530 BC. They conquered the dominant Tuatha Dé. All the royal clans of later Ireland were believed to have descended from the three sons of Miledh, Heremon, Heber and Ir.

How much of this is true, how much is fanciful, is difficult to determine. It is not improbable that the Milesians were in fact the Celts and that Spain designated any lands beyond the sea. If this is true then the ancient records would find support in archaeology.

The most interesting thing is that all these records of ancient times refer to men called Druids. Parthalón is said to have brought three Druids with him – the roots of their names mean Intelligence, Knowledge, Inquiry. The Nemedians had Druids who challenged the magic of the Fomorians by their own spells. The Druids of the Tuatha Dé Danann threw a cloud of darkness over the Druids of the Fir Bolg to enable their own people to settle in Ireland. While the Milesians were travelling to Ireland from Spain, their chief Druid, Caicher, told the people where they were going. 'What sort of place is Ireland?' asked the son of Agnomin, the chief. 'It is further than Scythia' the Druid replied, 'We ourselves will never reach it, but our descendants will in three hundred years time.'

The Red Branch Cycle (Craobh Ruadh)

The Heroic or Ulster Cycle of tales is concerned with the Ulster Heroes. They lived in a society typical of the Iron Age. The king was Conchobor mac Nessa. His great hall at Emain Macha was known as the *Craobh Ruadh*, and the stories concerning this group of tales is also known as the *Craobh Ruadh* or Red Branch Cycle of story-telling. Recent excavations at Emain Macha, which is near Armagh, have revealed a highly significant ceremonial site.

Conchobor's followers were called the Heroes of the Red Branch. *The Táin Bó Cúailnge* ('The Cattle Raid of Cooley') is the finest epic of this Cycle, and although it was probably written down in the seventh or eighth centuries, it would have been transmitted orally for several centuries before that. In all the sagas of the heroic age the Druids play a major rôle. There can be no doubt that the Druids so constantly mentioned in the early Irish sagas, no matter how imaginary may be, the events they describe, played a real part in early Irish civilisation, the main features of which can be discerned.

Cú Chulainn is the greatest hero in the Táin – nephew of the king, Conchobor mac Nessa. The young warrior protected Ulster against the combined might of the other four provinces of Ireland.

As a mere lad he got his weapons – two spears, shield and sword from Conchobor's Druid, Cathbad, Conchobor's father, in the earliest account. The Druid was teaching his pupils and said that the boy who took up arms on that day would be a champion amongst warriors, but would be short-lived although his fame would last forever.

The Second Battle of Moytura (Cath Maige Tuired)

The Second Battle of *Mag Tuired* (Moytura) is an account of the epic conflict between the Tuatha Dé Danann (People of the Goddess Danu) and the *Fomoire* (the Fomorians). These are the gods of pagan Ireland and their enemies, also in origin a supernatural race. The battle is set within the chronological framework of Irish pseudo-history represented by *Lebor Gabála Erénn* (The Book of Invasions of Ireland), and concerns the defence of Ireland by the gods. It is timeless and bears comparison with the great battles fought between Aesir and Vanir in Scandinavian mythology. It was known as the Second Battle to distinguish it from an earlier encounter between the Tuatha Dé Danann and the Fir Bolg. 'It is of great value for the comparative reconstruction of the Indo-European mythological inheritance as well as for the exploration of Irish mythological tradition itself' (Gray, 1982, 1). References to it are found throughout Irish literature, in learned tradition and epic narrative, bardic poetry and folklore. There are only two independent narrative versions of the battle, each represented by a single manuscript. The older version is based on Old Irish materials. Gray's version includes an edition of the whole narrative together with a translation that aims at completeness, and as well as being an excellent work of scholarship, it is a most important study.

The Harleian narrative, drawing together materials from a variety of sources, begins with events that take place long before the battle itself. While still living on islands to the north of Ireland the Tuatha Dé Danann ally themselves with the Fomoire, a demonic race, and Ethne, daughter of the Fomorian champion Balor, is given in marriage to Cian, son of the Tuatha Dé Danann physician, Dian Cécht. Soon afterwards, the Tuatha Dé Danann occupy Ireland. They overcome the previous inhabitants, the *Fir Bolg* in the first battle of Mag Tuired. In the course of the battle the Tuatha Dé king, Nuadu, loses an arm *(23)*, and thus cannot continue to rule. The king must be unblemished. The women of the Tuatha Dé wanted to elect Bres, illegitimate son of the Fomorian king Elatha and Ériu, a woman of the Tuatha Dé Danann. We next get the story of the conception of Bres. Eventually the Tuatha Dé agree to accept him as their king. Ériu was, of course, the eponymous goddess of Ireland. Bres' reign is disastrous: he has no concern for his people and seeks only his own gain. He ignores his subjects' proper rôles and status. Practitioners of the arts are given no recognition by him. The warrior, Ogma, is forced to provide the firewood. The Dagda ('the good god'), 'god

23 Nuadu, who lost his arm

of Druidism', master of its skills, is made to build *raths* (forts) for Bres. Moreover, he loses his ration of food to the extortionate *satirist*, Cridenbél. Advised by his son, the Mac Óg (Oengus), the Dagda destroys the satirist by means of his great greed; at the same time he causes Bres to utter a false judgement, and, after finishing the fortress for the king, chooses as a reward for his labour a single black heifer. We are not told the significance of this strange choice until the end of the story, when she leads home all the cattle taken from the Tuatha Dé as tribute.

Two distinct strands of narrative are now evident. In one the Tuatha Dé are immediately subject to demands for tribute from the Fomorian overlords, including Bres' father, Elatha. In the other, Lugh, the son of Cian and Ethne, arrives among the Tuatha Dé in the midst of this crisis and claims the right to enter the feast, which is restricted to practitioners of various arts, because he has a unique mastery of every skill and craft. Hearing of this, Nuadu invites Lugh to enter and after consultation with the tribe, makes him responsible for coordinating the coming battle of the gods. Lugh calls to him the representatives of all the arts in order to review their skills. He then sets the time for the battle and arranges for the provision of weapons. The story then turns to the crude adventures of the Dagda. It tells of his encounter with the Morrígan and their sexual union and her magical attack on the Fomorian king, Indech. While the preparations for battle proceed, Lugh sends the Dagda as ambassador to the Fomorians to gain a truce until Samain, 'Hallow E'en', the most dark and magical night of the year. The Fomorians mock the Dagda by giving him a gross meal, but he succeeds in his mission. He also gains the affection and Druidical help of Indech's daughter. Before the start of battle, the god Lugh questions each member of the Tuatha Dé regarding his or her particular skills and likely contribution to the impending conflict, thus revealing the superior skill and expertise of the tribe as a whole. He then asks the Druids what power they will bring to the battle, and they answer: 'Not hard to say. We will bring showers of fire on the faces of the Fomorians, so that they cannot look up, and the warriors contending with them can use their force to kill them.' Lugh, of course, is the all-skilled one, master of every art and craft and magical power. There is some preliminary skirmishing, and the ability of the Tuatha Dé to provide weapons and healing for the wounded astounds the Fomorians. They assign Rúadán, son of Bres and Brig (Brigit), daughter of the Dagda, to kill one of the craftsmen responsible. But it is Rúadán himself who is slain. However, the Fomorians are successful in destroying the Well of Healing of the Tuatha Dé. Despite this, the magical quality of Lugh's leadership and the effect of their unrivalled abilities in magical arts ultimately gives the victory to the outnumbered Tuatha Dé in spite of the loss of their king. The Tuatha Dé try to hold Lugh back from the battle lest he should come to harm. He escapes from their restraints and joins in the conflicts encouraging the Tuatha Dé by means of magic spells which he chants.

The turning point in the great battle is reached when he comes face to face with his maternal grandfather, and in the single combat which ensues, destroys Balor by casting a sling-stone at his Evil Eye. So he avenges the death of Nuadu. The battle then turns into a rout, as the Fomorians are driven back to the sea. The latter part of this dramatic and primitive tale consists of various negotiations between the Tuatha Dé and the vanquished Fomoire. Bres keeps his life in exchange for information which will lead to agricultural prosperity; the Dagda regains his stolen harp and harper, very magical possessions, by the subtle power of music rather than by force. The Tuatha Dé recover all the cattle taken as tribute by means of the lowing of the black heifer. Poets prophesy a new peace and prosperity for the Tuatha Dé in Ireland and victory is proclaimed. The final word however goes to the war-goddess the Morrígan who prophesies the end of all things, even the newly-won freedom acquired by the second battle of Mag Tuiredh. It is a dreadful, chilling poem, bleak and desolate and may echo the Druidic belief that although the world will never end, from time to time it will be overcome by water and by fire, a prophecy which would appear to be about to be substantiated at the present time.

Much of contemporary mythological analysis rests upon comparative, sociological and structural methods shaped by various scholars such as Émile Durkheim and Claude Levi-Strauss. These methods are especially applicable to Irish myths , where the world of the gods reflects the organisation of human society and illustrates the rôle of various social institutions in creating and maintaining social order.

One of the most important of these Structuralist scholars is Georges Dumézil whose studies of Indo-European tripartite systems have had a profound influence on many scholars, especially mythologists. There can be no doubt whatsoever about the extremely archaic elements in early Irish literary traditions, but in recent years the enthusiasm for Dumézil's hypotheses has, it would seem, lost some of its initial fervour. To me, personally, it seems that we have such a long way to go as yet in dealing with the vast amount of material available to us in the vernacular languages of the British Isles and Ireland, and so many texts to be edited for publication, that it is of greater use to canalise our energies and resources in this direction than to attempt over-ambitious programmes of comparative studies. Nevertheless, that does not prevent us from being aware of them, or from noting the apparent veracity of much of the work being carried out by scholars, many of whom are from the Continent of Europe. But until we have fully explored our own traditions from within our native cultures, Irish and British, it is going to be of less use to us than may be the case at a later state of our knowledge.

In view of the importance of this text I feel justified in including a fuller account of this unique saga. The language of the Second Battle of Moytura, then, reflects the Old Irish materials upon which the text is based, although it is a compilation that has been influenced considerably by Middle Irish scribes or redactors, especially with regard to its orthography. The language of the story is itself of considerable antiquity. It is basically of the ninth century: the tale is the Battle of Mag Tuired and the Birth of Bres son of Elatha and his Reign.

The Tuatha Dé Danann were in the northern islands of the world, studying occult lore and sorcery, Druidic arts and witchcraft and magical skills, until they surpassed the masters of all the pagan arts. They studied occult lore and secret knowledge and diabolic arts in four cities: Fálias, Gorias, Murias, and Findias. From Fálias was brought the Stone of Fál which was in Tara. It used to cry out beneath every rightful king of Ireland. From Gorias was brought Lugh's spear. No battle was ever sustained against it, or against the man who held it in his hand. From Findias was brought the sword of Nuadu. No one ever escaped from it once it was drawn from its deadly sheath, and no one could resist it. From Murias was brought the Dagda's cauldron. No company ever went away from it unsatisfied. There were four *Druids* in those four cities. Morfesa was in Fálias; Esras was in Gorias; Uiscias was in Findias; Semias was in Murias. Those are the four filidh from whom the Tuatha Dé learned occult lore and secret knowledge. (The Druids are called *Filidh*: an important point in connection with the fact that the Druids, Filidh and Bards were an all-inclusive priesthood.)

The Tuatha Dé then made an alliance with the Fomoire, and Balor the grandson of Nét gave his daughter Ethne to Cian the son of Dian Cécht. And she bore the gifted child, Lugh.

The Tuatha Dé came to Ireland with a great fleet to take it by force from the Fir Bolg. Upon reaching the territory of Corcu Belgatan (identified with Sliab Maccu Belgodon, in an area near Cong, Co. Mayo, the site of the First Battle of Mag Tuired), they at once burned their boats so that they would not think of escaping in them. The smoke and the mist which came from the ships filled the land and the air which was near them. For that reason it had been thought they had arrived in clouds of mist. The first battle was fought between them and the Fir Bolg.

The Fir Bolg were defeated by the Tuatha Dé Danann. Their king, Eochaidh mac Eirc, was also slain. It was in the battle that Nuadu's arm was cut off. Dian Cécht, the physician, aided by Crédne the brazier, made for him a hand of silver that had the same powers of movement as a real hand. Many men of the Tuatha

Dé were killed in that battle. Those Fir Bolg who escaped from the battle with their lives made for the lands of the Fomoire and settled in Arran and Islay, in Man and Rathlin. Nuadu's injury had rendered him unfit for kingship of the Tuatha Dé (all kings must be unblemished) and there was a great deal of dissension over who should take his place. Eventually it was decided to give the sovereignty to Bres, son of Elatha, who was their adopted son.

This is the story of his conception: one day a woman of the Tuatha Dé, Ériu (or Éri) was gazing over the land and the sea when she saw a silver vessel seemingly of great size coming towards the land on the glass smooth sea. A fine man with long golden hair came towards her, wearing a cloak banded with golden thread. His shirt was likewise embroidered in gold. He wore a brooch of gold with a glowing precious stone set into it; he had two spears of bright silver with shafts of bronze. Around his neck were five circlets of gold. He had a gold-hilted sword inlaid with silver and with studs of gold. He requested an hour of love-making with her. She replied that she had made no such tryst with him. 'Come without the trysting' he said. So they lay down together. Later, as the stranger got up, she began to weep. He asked her why she was weeping. The woman replied that it was for two reasons that she wept, the first being that they should part when they had only just met and the second cause for sorrow was that although the young men of the Tuatha Dé Danann had all been courting her in vain, she had succumbed to him, a stranger. He told her not to worry about that and took the gold ring off his middle finger and gave it to her. He instructed her never to part with the ring except to one whose finger it would fit. 'I am also concerned because I do not know who you are'. He told her that he was Elatha, son of Delbaith, king of the Fomoire. He also told her that their love-making would result in the birth of a son who must be named Eochu Bres (Eochu the Beautiful). His beauty would be unrivalled.

The boy was duly born. His growth was phenomenal; at seven years he was the size of a fourteen-year-old lad, and so on until he was fourteen years old. The sovereignty of Ireland was given to him. He took an oath that he would renounce his rule if he did not behave in a kingly manner. His sureties were seven Druids, seven Filidh and seven chieftains. His mother gave land to him and he had a fortress put up on it, built by the Dagda, 'the Good God'. This was because after Bres had taken over the kingship of Ireland the Fomorians became aggressive and hostile and exacted taxes and tribute from all the people.

The warriors of Ireland were reduced to servitude by them. Ogma, god of eloquence, had to carry great bundles of firewood and the Dagda was reduced to building forts. The Dagda was made wretched by this slavery and his situation was made worse by the satirist, Cridenbél, a blind man who resented the size of the Dagda's meals in comparison with his own portions. He threatened the Dagda with his powers of satire while demanding the three best pieces of each serving he received. Fear of satire was great and so the Dagda could not do anything except concur with his demands. Sadly, the portions of the satirist were huge, each the size of a fine pig. This soon began to affect the Dagda's looks.

One day he was working in a trench when he saw the Mac Óc ('Young Son'), a god of the Tuatha Dé, the Dagda's son, whose real name was Oengus, coming towards him. The young god asks his father what is making him look so ill. The Dagda tells him the whole tale. The Mac Óc listens carefully and then tells his father how to rid himself of the oppressor. He gives him three gold coins and tells him to put them into the three portions of food which are given to Cridenbél in the evening. This he does and his enemy dies. He himself is threatened with death, but he tells the king the truth, the coins are found in the satirist's stomach, and the Dagda is spared. When the Dagda went to work next day his son again came to him to advise him not to ask for any payment for his labours which are almost completed. 'Ask for the cattle of Ireland to be brought to you. Choose from among them the dark, black-maned, trained, spirited heifer.'

The Dagda finished his labours and Bres asked him what he wanted as wages for his work. The Dagda replied: 'I would like you to gather the cattle of Ireland together in one place.' Bres did as he had been asked, and the Dagda chose the heifer from among them as his son had advised him. The king thought this was stupid, since the Dagda could have chosen a much higher wage. Nuadu, who had lost his arm in battle, was receiving treatment from the physician, Dian Cécht, who had created a silver hand for him, which could move like a living hand, but that did not please his son Miach and he went to the hand, and he recited a charm which was still used in the Hebrides in the nineteenth century: 'Joint to joint, and sinew to sinew' – this was frequently employed as a magical spell to heal cattle or other stock that had injured themselves. Miach healed the arm in nine days and nine nights, a magical number. For the first three days, Nuadu carried the arm against his side, and the skin grew over it. For the second three days, he held it against his chest. For the third three days, Miach used an ancient magical spell; he would cast wisps of bulrushes after they had been blackened in a fire; the casting of straws or wisps for magical purposes occurs in several early Irish contexts and it also figures in Gaelic folklore.

His father, however, did not like that cure. He hurled a sword at the crown of Miach's head and cut his scalp to the bone. Miach healed it by means of his skill. His father struck him again, cutting him more deeply; Miach healed it by the same means. His father struck the third blow and it went through the bone. Miach healed this likewise, but the fourth blow cut out the brain and Miach died, and Dian Cécht said that no healer could cure him. Then his father buried Miach and 365 herbs grew through the grave, equalling the number of his joints and sinews; but Dian Cécht came and mixed up the herbs so that nobody understood their healing properties.

The Tuatha Dé Danann tried to drive Bres from the kingship because his rule was unjust and the land and the people were suffering. He asked to remain king for seven years and the assembly agreed, imposing certain terms on him. Hoping to outwit the Tuatha Dé Danann, he went to his mother and asked where his kinsmen dwelt. She gave him the ring which had been left with her by his father. When he put it on his middle finger, it fitted him. No one else could wear it. His father recognised the ring and asked who the warrior was. His mother answered, and told him that Bres was his son. 'Why have you come?' asked his father. 'To ask you for warriors', he said. 'I shall take that land by force.' His father said that he should not attempt to take the land if he could not take it by just means. 'What is your advice, then?' said Bres. Nuadu was once again king of the Tuatha Dé Danann and this is when the great god Lugh came to Tara, the seat of the king.

The Tuatha Dé Danann were victorious after a gory battle, in which many died or were horribly wounded. It is to the Morrígan, the war goddess, that heads severed in the battle were offered. The Morrígan then chants a grim prophecy about the end of the world, describing every deadly disease and evil that would occur:

> I shall not see a world
> Which will be dear to me:
> Cattle without milk,
> Women with no modesty
> Men without courage
> Conquests with no king
> Woods without oak-mast
> Sea without produce
> False judgments of aged men
> False pleadings of lawyers
> Every man a traitor
> Every son dishonourable
> Families will succumb to incest
> An evil time. Son will cheat his father
> Daughter will deceive.

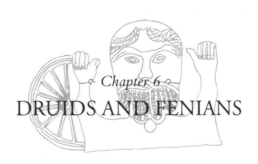

—⊱ *Chapter 6* ⊰—
DRUIDS AND FENIANS

Druids were an integral part of Celtic society and it is therefore essential to consider them, their origins, evolution, and general rôle in that society in order to assess their significance and primary nature. Celtic society was, of course, tribally organised, and the Druids – who were themselves of noble birth – functioned as a rule from within that society. There was, however, by about the third century AD, another element which existed outwith the established, settled society, but the members (who were not outcasts or écland) of which could by reason of their noble origins, attain Druidic status. The initiated of this non-tribal society were organised into groups or bands of warriors, each one with a distinctive leader. The most famous of these leaders was Fionn (or Finn) mac Cum(h)aill, leader of the Fian of Leinster. Fian or Fianna connoted a war-band or war-bands. The anglicised term for Fianna is Fenians. These groups roamed the countryside and are represented as being the defenders of Ireland against foreign invaders. Fionn's birth is of interest. His father Cumaill wanted to marry Muirne, who was the daughter of Tadg, the king's chief Druid. The king resented the union, which was against his wishes, and he sent an army against Cumaill. In the ensuing battle, Cumaill was killed. His wife fled and in due course gave birth to Fionn. Tadg was the son of the god Nuadu and the Fenian Cycle of Stories has thus a strongly mythological aspect.

Thus Fionn had the god Nuadu as his grandfather and is generally considered to be a manifestation of the pan-Celtic god Lugh.
Sometimes his name occurs as Findlug, and other gods play some
rôle in the Fenian legends. The Fenians were subject to the authority of their own leaders, not to that of the tribe. Their origin is
described in a fascinating collection of stories which may date to
the twelfth century but clearly originated in a much older Celtic
milieu. Known as *Agallamh na Senórach* ('The Colloquy of the Old
Men') it is a long and elaborate composition which may be
regarded as a framework for numerous tales of heroism and the
source of place-names connected with Fionn and his followers.
The name of the place is used to raise the question as to why it was
so named and answered by a story of Fenian valour. These tales are
often of considerable length and complexity. The popularity of the
leader was widespread and he appears in the Welsh Triads as Ffin
fab Kael. It is a colourful and invaluable compilation. Stories of the
Fenians were treasured by the people of the land whereas those of
the Mythological Cycle and the great Ulster Cycle would seem to
have been favoured by the more sophisticated nobles of the Irish
tribes. This is a generalisation however, based in the main on the
fact that the Fenian texts were committed to writing at a fairly late
period. Nevertheless, fragments of the other Cycles have certainly
found their way into the oral tradition and been recorded by
collectors in Ireland and Gaelic Scotland, where they were
extremely popular. Some of these can still be heard at the present
time.

What then was the difference between the Tuatha Dé Danann,
and the Fenians? It is useful to consider how the Fenians originated and the nature of their society which lived *outside* the tribal
system. First, however, it may be mentioned that, although the
Fenians were accredited with great length of life, they did eventually die: they could also be killed in full strength, frequently in
battle; by a wild animal, or through some other mishap. It was a
Druidic belief, the central belief perhaps, that death was not the
end of life, merely a stage in a long existence to which there was

no foreseeable end, only many rebirths in different shapes and forms, sometimes human, sometimes animal or avian.

An unusually interesting illustration of this doctrine occurs in the story of Mongan mac Fiachna. He was known as the son of the seventh-century king, Fiachna Lurga, but this was not, in fact, the case. Aedan son of Gabran was involved in a war in Scotland and he sent a message to Fiachna to come to his aid as things were going against him. Meanwhile, a man of noble countenance came to his queen who had remained at Fiachna's stronghold. There were few people about at the time and the handsome stranger asked the queen to arrange a time when they could come together. The queen was shocked at his proposition and said that nothing in the world would make her unfaithful to her husband. When he asked her if she was not willing to save his life, she replied that if it was in danger then she would do anything to help him. He told her that the king was indeed in great danger. A terrible warrior had been brought to fight with him and he would surely be killed. If the queen consented to make love with him a son would be born of that union; his name would be Mongan and his fame would be great. He would go to the battle which was to be fought next day at the third hour, and he himself would save the king 'before the eyes of the men of Scotland'. He said he would tell her husband of their union to which she had consented only because she wished his life to be spared. And so it was done. Next day when the opposing armies were drawn up for battle, a fine, noble-looking man was seen before the army of Fiachna and Aedan. He told Fiachna what had happened and then he went to the opposing warriors and overcame them all and Fiachna and Gabran won the day.

Fiachna then returned to his stronghold and his wife became pregnant and in due course bore a son who was known as Mongan, son of Fiachna. Fiachna felt only gratitude to his wife for the way in which she had saved his life. The father of the child was, in fact, the god, Manannán mac Lir, who remained a popular figure in story and tradition down to modern times in the Celtic regions. The Isle of Man is allegedly named after him. He was primarily a god of the sea; his name, *ler* means 'sea, ocean'. Before he departed, the stranger had left a verse with her which said 'I go home, the pale pure morning draws near; Manannán son of Lir is the name of him who comes to thee'.

Many stories are told about Mongan who was probably a divinity himself, bearing in mind his divine father. Of particular interest to the survival down the centuries of at least certain Druidic precepts and ideas is the tale which is entitled 'A Story from which it is inferred that Mongan was Finn Mac Cumhaill'. The following is a précis of the tale: Mongan had succeeded his father and was now king of the province. Forgall was his poet. He used to recite a tale to Mongan every night. His repertoire of lore and tradition was so great that the king was listening to the poet from Samuin (1 November) to Bealtain (1 May). In return, the poet received gifts and food from the king, as was customary. One day Mongan asked Forgall to tell him about the death of Fothadh Airgdech. The poet claimed that he was killed at Duffry in Leinster. Mongan said he was wrong. The poet said he would satirise him with his opprobrious poems and he would likewise satirize his father and his mother *and* his grandfather. Moreover, he would chant spells upon their waters so that no fish would be caught in the estuaries. He would sing upon their woods which would yield no crops of fruit; he would chant spells on the plains and so render them barren for ever.

The great power of the poet, well-attested both in the classics and in the vernacular literatures in general, is shown by the fear and dread which these threats occasioned. Mongan offered the poet more and more and he was unmoved; he offered him half of his kingdom then the whole kingdom, but Forgall remained obdurate. The poet finally refused to accept anything in return for the removal of his terrible satire except his wife. For the sake of his honour the king had to accede to this. Mongan had, however, only agreed to part with his wife if help did not come to him before the end of three days. His poor wife wept and was wretched as the days passed by and the third day dawned. The poet then began to demand his reward. Mongan begged him to wait until the evening of the day. He and his wife were in their summer-house, she weeping pitifully. Suddenly the king said 'Do not grieve; I hear the footsteps of the man who is coming to save us.'Time passed and no one came.The king told his wife to stop weeping for he could hear the steps of the one who would help them and they were coming nearer. They were like this all day, the queen weeping and her husband trying to comfort her by saying he could hear the footsteps of their rescuer drawing ever nearer.Then night began to fall. Mongan was on his couch in the palace and his wife was at his right hand, lamenting.The poet was enumerating their sureties and their bonds to him. Suddenly the watchman came and announced the approach of a stranger coming from the south. His cloak was folded about him and he carried a great headless spear-shaft in his hand. Using this shaft he leapt across the three ramparts and landed in the middle of the enclosure and from there into the middle of the palace where Mongan was reclining on his couch. The poet stood behind the king. He asked what was wrong and the king answered saying 'I and that poet made a wager about the death of Fothadh Airgdech.The poet said it occurred at Duffry in Leinster. I replied that he was wrong.The strange warrior said the poet was wrong.' 'It shall be proved.We were with thee, with Fionn' said the warrior. 'Be quiet' said Mongan, 'that is not fair.' 'We were with Fionn, then,' said the stranger, 'We came from Scotland. We met with Fothadh Airgdech on the River Larne. We fought a battle there. I made a cast at him and my spear passed right through him and into the earth beyond, and it left its iron head in the earth. Here then is the shaft that belonged to that spear.The stone from which I made that cast, and the spear-head in the earth will both be found.The tomb of Fothadh Airgdech is a little to the east of it. He lies in the earth in a stone chest. Lying on his breast are his two silver bracelets and his two arm-rings, and his torc of silver. Beside his tomb stands a stone pillar. On the end of the pillar is an inscription in Ogam, saying 'This is Fothadh Airgdech. Cáilte slew me in an encounter against Fionn.' They went there with the warrior. Everything was found as the stranger had described it.The warrior who had come to them was Cáilte, Fionn's foster-son. Mongan was Fionn 'though he would not let it be told'.

In this story we have a nice assemblage of archaic motifs which we meet time and again in tales and poems of all periods of the Irish tradition. Here we have Mongan, son of the god Manannán in this life but the great hero Fionn mac Cumhaill in a previous existence. His powers enable him to call up his friend Cailte, one of the foremost of the Fenian warriors in Fionn's own time. He is then able to testify to the truth of the argument with the powerful poet and so save the queen from being given to him. The great powers of satire and the satirist are fully-attested, especially the poet's ability to destroy natural features and phenomena with his excessive demands. It is not surprising that the poet and his powers were universally feared for the poet could literally 'make' his lord famous, and therefore had considerable influence over him. On the other hand, his satire was terrible; it could cause blemishes and even death if he were to be displeased, with, for example, his payment for services rendered.

The classical commentators on the Celts understood and commented upon the great and sinister powers of this class of Celtic poet, no matter what he was offered by way of atonement. The classics knew and commented on the great powers of the satirist; all the Celtic literatures were familiar with his intimidating and dangerous magic. He could literally make or break his patron. This fear of the satirical powers of the poet has survived to the present day when the poet is still universally respected and is also regarded as possessing powers of satire in the Celtic-speaking countries and areas. In the early Irish laws, one of the poet's most important functions seems to have been to satirise and to praise. His status was very high, and a person's 'honour-price' could be damaged through satire and increased through praise. The alleged power of the Irish poets to 'rhyme to death' both men and animals, especially rats, is frequently referred to in English sources from the sixteenth century onwards. The poet's powers were not only used for destructive purposes; legal commentary reveals that the chief poet *(ollam)* should always remain in the king's presence in order to protect him from sorcery. The poet, likewise, is often accredited with powers of prophecy similar to those of the Druids. According to one legal tract, the Fili derives his status from three skills: *imbas forosna* ('encompassing knowledge which illuminates'), *teinm laeda* ('breaking of marrow') and *dichetal do chennaib*, ('chanting by means of heads'). In spite of such pagan associations, the poets were clearly a wealthy and influential group in early Irish society; but, if he was fraudulent through overcharging, not prophesying correctly, or producing a bad poem he lost his *nemed* ('free') status. The poet had very considerable powers: he had the right to cross all boundaries and therefore he must have had quite a wide influence and mixed considerably with members of other tribes. The highest grade of poet was the *ollam*, who had the same honour-price as the king of a *tuath* ('tribe') (See Kelly 1988).

Fionn and his followers were known as a *Fian*; each member of a Fian was a *féinnidh*. There were several groups of this kind, under their own individual leaders, but that of Fionn was the most famous and they became the focus for innumerable tales and legends. The Fenians were not members of this marginal society by birth. They achieved such status by means of a series of daunting and perilous ordeals which must be undergone and overcome. Some examples of these are as follows. A large hole was dug, deep enough to reach up to the waist of the candidate who had to enter it equipped with his shield and a hazel stick as long as his arm. Then nine warriors bearing nine spears and standing at a distance of ten furrows away from the candidate must attack him and cast their spears at him simultaneously. If he were to be wounded, he would not be taken into the *Fian*. No one was accepted until his hair had been braided and he began to run through the woodlands of Ireland. Those who sought to wound him came after him. There was only a single branch of a tree between them when they started. Were he to be overtaken by his pursuers he would be wounded and would not be received into Fianship. If his weapons had trembled in his hands he would be rejected. If a branch in the wood had pulled any of the hair from its braids he would not be accepted. If, in running, he had cracked a dry stick under his feet he was no longer eligible for Fianship. He must be able to jump over a stick that was level with his forehead and pass under one at the same level as his knee while running at full speed. And, still running at great speed and without slowing down at all he must be able to remove a thorn from his foot with his nail. Having fulfilled all these harsh requirements he is ready to be taken into Fianship.

Over and above these physical ordeals, and most importantly, the *féinid*-elect must be highly-educated. He must be thoroughly versed in the 12 traditional forms of poetry; all the Fenian warriors were poets. This required 7 to 12 years of training. Some also claimed to be Druids, which would involve up to 20 years of intensive and difficult oral study. The classics tell us that it took some seven years to become a qualified bard; some twelve years to become a file; and twenty years to become a Druid. All learning was of an oral nature. In the episode of the gigantic Laighne, Fionn claimed that he and his companions were 'all Druids'. The learned orders were exempt from fighting; all borders and boundaries were open to them. Yet the Fenians were both learned and great warriors.

Once the candidate had been accepted as a *féinid* he must sever all connections with his own people or clan. Thus no member of his clan might claim compensation for his death or injury; he was under no obligation to avenge wrongs done to his clan.

We have then in Ireland, at this early, pre-Christian period, a strange situation according to the Irish tradition. Two mythical races inhabit the land co-terminously; the gods of Ireland, the Tuatha Dé Danann, with their own warriors and bards, filid and Druids; and the Fenians. They come into contact from time to time, but appear on the whole to live quite independently of one another. Both are of divine or semi-divine origin, gods or warrior-magicians; the Tuatha Dé more so than the Fenians. However Fionn, for example, a god himself, is related to great deities, his father being Cumhall, thought to be the British war-god Camulos (but this is not now always accepted). He has close affinities with the British deity, Gwynn ap Nudd and with Nuadha, king of the Tuatha Dé Danann. He is also associated with Arthur of Britain and the story of *Culhwch and Olwen* of Welsh tradition has parallels with the Fenian legends. Both the Arthur cycle and the Fionn cycle were known and acclaimed throughout Europe, Arthur's exploits becoming known there from the twelfth century onwards, and the legends of Fionn in written form in the eighteenth century due to MacPherson's influence. Nennius, in the ninth century calls Arthur *dux bellorum* which is virtually equivalent to the title of Fionn as *righfhéinid*.

The division of Ireland

The Fenians did not retreat into the wilderness of Ireland because they had no other choice. They did so because they loved it and the life which it offered. How did this come about? Once there was a king of Ireland called Feradach Fechtnach. He had two sons. The story of the division of Ireland between them is told in *Agallamh na Senórach* (The Colloquy of the old Men). Caoilte, the swift-footed runner, tells the Christian noblemen of a later age about the division made by the two sons of Feradach. One of them was happy to take the wealth and the treasures, the herds and the dwelling houses and fortresses; the other preferred the estuaries and the cliffs, the wild fruits of the countryside and the sea, the many-coloured salmon and the game. Those listening said this was no fair division and that the first son had taken by far the richest half of Ireland. But Caoilte disagreed with this saying that the portion that they had agreed to was the one that he and the others, his Fenian companions, much preferred. So both brothers, in fact, got the portion each desired.

According to Nagy, J., 1955, p.13, '... To study the Fenian tradition is to touch the heart of Gaelic culture. The overwhelming popularity of the Fenian tales in Gaelic-speaking areas in Ireland

24 Stone figure found on
Cathedral Hill, Armagh,
Northern Ireland, 'radiate god'
cult object 69 cm high

and Scotland over the past several centuries attests to the validity of this claim. Furthermore, the Fenian tradition offers us a Celtic glimpse into the ideological heritage of the Indo-European peoples. In this tradition we find vivid manifestations of Indo-European concepts concerning the function of poets and the origins of poetic inspiration.'

A eulogy by Caoilte, one of the Fenian warriors:

> ... our noble leader rich in hosts, our wonderful sage, gifted in many ways, our lord, our skilled one, our seer, our judge, our wise man, our Druid, our head of strength, our trail of the host, Finn son of Cumhall son of Trenmor.

The subject of the Fenians is a huge one, especially as their popularity continued down the ages in the lore of the people leaving a vast corpus of material to be collected. Much must have perished without trace and it is becoming less and less easy to find tradition-bearers who have genuine Fionn lore today. But they *do* exist.

Fionn gained his magic knowledge by tasting the Salmon of Wisdom as it was being cooked. His wife was a deer called Saar. When her child was born, he had a tuft of deer-hair on his brow because she had licked him, although she had been warned not to do so. Therefore his name was *Oisín* ('little deer'). Fionn's dogs were in fact his nephews in animal form. Their mother was turned into a bitch.

Fionn had a magic hood which turned him into dog, man or deer, according to which way he wore it. This is a very archaic belief. There is a family in the Hebrides which believes that it is directly descended from seals. A seal was their progenitor. When I was living there, I was told that they could never hurt or kill a seal because they were their relatives. Fionn could turn himself into any animal. There are many surviving tales and legends of this kind in Ireland and Gaelic Scotland.

I am recounting the following tale in full because it demonstrates that there was a high standard of learning amongst these Wilderness dwellers, and some of them at least became fully qualified Druids.

Fionn and Laighne

Laighne, monstrous son of the king of the terrible Fomorians, a demonic race, came upon Fionn, king of the Fian of Ireland and his warriors who were gathered in full assembly in Dun Bó. Their main function was to protect the land of Ireland from invasion. They had hardly been there when they could see the huge Fomorian warrior coming towards them. He had crossed over from Scotland, his boat – which he rowed single-handed – creating great waves on the sea. No one of the Fenians had dared to put to sea for three years past for fear of the huge man and his powerful

vessel. The Fomorian made straight for the haven the Fenians were
guarding. His sword was a great club of hard iron with 300 iron
knobs on one of its sides. When the huge man came to land he
gave out a blood-curdling roar; the Fomorian was seeking battle –
conflict of warriors.

The Fenians quickly took council and Fionn, who was daunted
by nothing, said he would go straight to the Fomorian's tent *(pubal)*
in the guise of a poet (which he was!). Wise Fionn, with three
others made for the fine tent of the Fomorian king's only son.
Fionn, the bold leader with Fergus of the sweet voice, greeted the
huge man. They had never in all their lives seen anyone to equal
that warrior. He seated himself in his tent in honour of the four
poets. Fionn and Fergus sat beside him and Fionn put his cloak
round Cú Dhearoil and Blathnaid.

They played that soft, soothing music to which the Druids used
to sing a song. Then the son of hospitable Cumhall asked the fearsome warrior to tell him his true name and the name of his destination. Significantly the stranger addresses Fionn as *'A dhraoi uasail
iodhain'* – 'O noble, undefiled *Druid*'. He revealed that he was the
son of the Fomorian king in the east. 'As I do battle with all cham-
pions, my name is Laighne Mor, 'Great Laighne'. Courageous
Fionn then asked the giant why he left the east 'to come to delightful, fish-abounding Ireland?'. The unsuspecting warrior replied 'I
will tell you that, pure and noble Druid.' He then revealed that he
had come so that the nobles of Ireland might become subservient
to him and pay him a tribute annually or else no potent man
capable of fathering children should be allowed to remain in pure
Ireland. Fionn replied that many heroes had come to Ireland in
search of battle and not one of them returned to his dwelling in the
east. Laighne said he would yield his seat to no one out of fear of
warrior battle. Oisín then asked his brave Druids 'What payment do
you consider worthy, oh pure and worthy Druids?'

'You shall get gold and silver and everything you wish for.' 'We
are Druids full of wisdom,' said Fionn in reply, 'you owe us reverence; I ask for that by all you hold honourable'. The great man

promised to give that proper reverence to people of learning. He said that as long as he lived he would not harm any poet. 'You swear to that?' said Fionn son of Cumhall, 'Swear to respect honourably as long as you live all that we own of Ireland'. Laighne swore an oath that for all time he would never in his life ask any Druid who visited his house to pay any kind of tax or levy. Then Fionn revealed the trick he had played on the huge, brutal warrior. 'You would be as well to return from where you have come. Your journey is completed. Ireland belongs to me. I am Fionn, prince of the true Fian.' 'If you are Fionn of the Fian,' said the generous warrior, 'I swore no oath to anyone but learned Druids.' 'I am a Druid, brave warrior', said Fionn, 'my skill has never been surpassed by anyone who has walked this dewy world.' Fionn, by his courage and his Druidry has overcome a feared and monstrous foe. His cunning and his courage amaze the giant Fomorian who acknowledges defeat and makes generous terms with the warrior-Druid and his fellows.

The Fenian legends thus belong to a very archaic, perhaps Indo-European tradition. They have survived even to this day amongst the people and I have heard many stories of them myself in the Highlands and Islands of Scotland.

Chapter 7

ASSEMBLIES AND
CALENDAR FESTIVALS

The Gauls all assert their descent from Dis pater and say that it is the Druidic belief. For this reason they count periods of time not by the number of days but by the number of nights; and in reckoning birthdays and the new moon and new year their unit of reckoning is the night followed by the day. In the rest of their way of life, nearly their sole difference from other peoples is that they do not allow their sons to approach them in public unless they have grown up to the age of military service, and they think it is a disgrace for a boy under this age to sit in public within sight of his father.

(Caesar, *De Bello Gallico*, VI, 18)

Archaeology and tradition

The Celts in Gaul and in the British Isles, also in Galatia and probably Iberia *(25)* used to hold festive assemblies under the aegis of the king and his Druids. The festivals might take place annually or at other regular intervals, such as three or five years. They were: *Samain* (Hallowe'en: the most fraught and ominous of the festivals), on 1 November; *Imbolc*, the day the ewes were believed to begin lactating, on 1 February; *Beltain*, a joyous festival heralding the beginning of Summer, on 1 May;

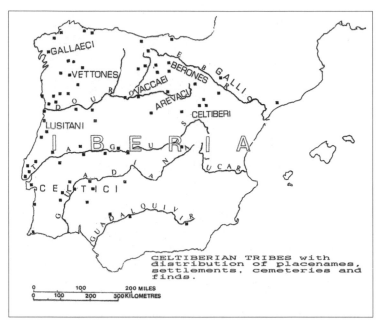

25 Celtiberian tribes, with the distribution of Celtic placenames,
settlements, cemeteries and finds

and lastly *Lughnasa*, the feast of the god Lugus, the first-fruit festival on 1 August. In Ireland, the main purpose of these great gatherings, which were in honour of the gods, tended to be
concerned primarily with feasting and other forms of pleasure
such as horse racing and recitation of the tribal lore and history,
chanted by the bards. They were essentially for the good of the
land and the stock according to the season. It is likely that some,
at least, of the assembly sites were associated with graves of
venerated ancestors, or the cult site of some god or goddess.

We can only surmise in a general way as to what actually took
place at these assemblies in pre-Christian times, but in a very
valuable Irish record of the meaning of the names of places and
the stories attached to them – *Dindshenchas* ('Stories of Eminent

1 *Left* Coin of the Iceni/Eceni, silver, 70–50 BC; malevolent female wearing diadem and faced by double-ram-headed snake; probably Andraste, the goddess of Queen Boudica. 2 *Right* Three-headed bust of Celtic deity, Condat, Cantal, France

3 Bronze ritual crown, Hockwold-cum-Wilton, Norfolk, England

4 Bronze boar from the probable Druid sanctuary at Neuvy-en-Sullias, Loiret, France

SOUTHERN GAUL
silver

VIDUCASSES
gold

5 *Left* Bronze stag, Neuvy-en-Sullias, Loiret, France

6 *Below* Bronze head of carnyx, Deskford, Grampian, Scotland

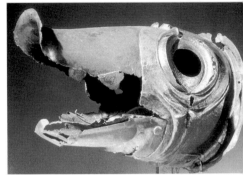

7 *Left* Bronze knob-horned head from Warwickshire, England: compare horns of Nuadu in *fig. 23* (p.119)

8 *Right* Relief of mother goddesses, Cirencester, Gloucestershire, England

9 *Left* Stone head from Yorkshire, England. *Courtesy Chris Rudd.* 10 Stone head from Yorkshire, England. *Courtesy Chris Rudd*

11 *Left* Stone head from Yorkshire, England. *Courtesy Chris Rudd.* 12 *Right* Stone head mounted on stone base, Corleck, Co. Cavan, Ireland

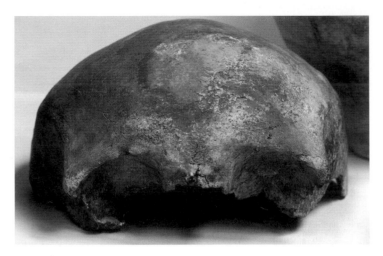

13 Skull, Coventina's Well, Northumberland, England

14 *Left* Cult figure, stone, from site of early church, now at Blackness Castle, Midlothian, Scotland. 15 *Centre* Three-horned bull, Autun, Saône-et-Loire, France. 16 *Right* Bronze figure of a druid, Neuvy-en-Sullias, Loiret, France

17 *Left* Miniature votive shield, from the Salisbury Hoard, Wiltshire, England
18 *Right* Shrine, Tigh a' Cailliche, Glen Lyon, Perthshire, Scotland

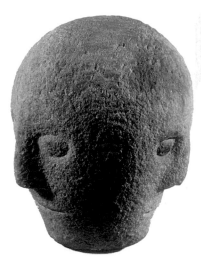

19 Stone tricephalos, Corleck, Co. Cavan, Ireland

20 *Above* Janiform stone heads with a raptor's beak between them, Roquepertuse, Bouches-du-Rhône, France

21 *Left* Bronze figure of a god in characteristic Buddhic pose and wearing a torc; found in a bog at Bouray, Seine-et-Oise, France

24 *Opposite below* Bronze fleshfork or divining rod, with swans and ravens, both of which were birds of omen; Dunaverney, Co. Antrim, Northern Ireland

22 Right
Arduina riding
a boar, Jura,
France

23 Left Dea Artio
with a bear, the
proportions of
which imply it is
her attribute and
transformation
shape; Berne,
Switzerland

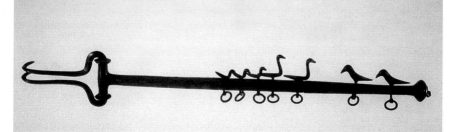

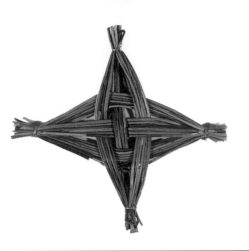

25 *Above* St Brigit's crosses of straw; Ireland

26 *Left* Massive silver torc, weight 6kg, for wear by an idol, found on the 'east' bank of the River Neckar, Kr. Rottweil, near Stuttgart, Germany. The bulls wear torcs

27 *Below left* Sandstone head of the one-eyed Celtic deity known in Ireland as Balor, found near Water Newton, Cambridgeshire, England. *Courtesy Rupert Wace*

Places') – there is a poem of some eighty-one four-line stanzas, which concerns the Assembly at Carman (on the plain called the *Curragh* of Kildare). Several verses describe the actual proceedings; in translation they read:

> *(Verse 2)* Carman, site of generous Fair,
> Smooth the lawn for coursing there;
> Hosts who sought its trysting-place
> Conquered in its brilliant race

> *(Verse 30)* These the pledges: that the Fair,
> Every third year gathered there,
> By no strife disturbed, should be
> Held in solemn harmony.

> *(Verse 53)* When the harvest month began
> After lapse of three years' span,
> Daily seeking victors' praise,
> Riders raced through seven days.

> *(Verse 54)* Settlement of tax and due,
> Legal cases to review,
> Laws to publish and declare –
> This the business of the Fair.

> *(Verse 59)* Here is music – trumpet *(26)*, horn,
> Drum and pipe the Fair adorn:
> Here is poetry – the bard
> Seeks and gains his due reward.

> *(Verse 60)* Here romance – exhaustless theme!
> Legends, vague as in a dream:
> Here is wisdom – proverbs sage,
> Satires, lore of seer and mage. [*magus*, Druid]

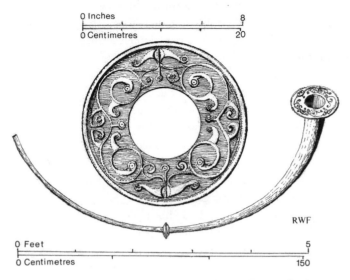

26   Trumpet, Lough-na-Shade, Co Armagh, Northern Ireland

(Verse 62) Here is history – tales of old,
Ever new, though often told,
Annals, conquests, wooings, strife,
Love and hatred, death and life.

(Verse 65) But what noisy rabble's there,
On the border of the Fair? –
Vagabonds with drums and bones,
Shrieking to their bagpipe-drones

Because our documentary evidence is more prolific for Ireland, but less early in date, it may well have been that the aspect of the assembly which took precedence amongst the Continental Celts was the business of running the affairs of the tribes in general, for example, at the great annual assembly at Chartres, centred in the land of the tribe of the Carnutes from which the name Chartres is derived. People travelled from all over the country to bring legal actions and disputes of various kinds for adjudication by the Druids. Boundary disputes were always troublesome and often led to internecine strife and even bloodshed. Boundary customs were numerous and many survive to the present day. The king and his Druids would sit in judgment at the hearings of these and many other matters. The Druids would have presided over the inevitable sacrifices which were an essential part of worship and of ensuring the goodwill of the gods, with whom only the Druids could communicate directly.

The classical writers comment: 'for they [Druids] alone know the will of the gods'. On the basis of such Irish evidence as we possess, it would be likely that once the more serious cases had been disposed of, the people would be free to enjoy the festivities. As these must have been gatherings on a very large scale it is not hard to imagine the amount of organisation that would have been necessary to provide some form of shelter (perhaps pavilions or tents) together with huge cauldrons of food and vats of alcoholic liquor. Entertainment would include poetic recitation, the playing of musical instruments *(plate 6)*, and, of course, horse-racing contests and sports such as hurley. We may perhaps have some echo of these in the Highland Games of the present time, which draw crowds from all over the world.

The present-day cathedral of Chartres stands out from the great plain which dominates that region of France, Eure-et-Loire. Both church and plain are of considerable interest. Plains, in general (Gaulish *magus*, Irish *magh*, Welsh *maes*) were amongst the natural features most revered by the Druids and the fact that in the centre of this plain, one of the finest cathedrals in France was erected is significant in view of several features which can be associated directly with pagan Celtic religion, and thus with the Druids themselves. In the centre of such sacred plains there was invariably an ancient tree, which was imbued with a great sanctity and formed the focal point for meetings. It was known as *bile* in Old Irish, and place-names on the Continent − including

Bilum in Denmark and Bilem in France – suggest that it served as an *axis mundi* (world tree – cf. Scandinavian *yggdrasil*).

When the cathedral was under construction, a wooden image of a goddess was found and was taken as a sign that a church should be erected on this spot. The image was, however, of a pagan mother-goddess and many such have been recovered from sites in various parts of France and became known as *Viérges Noirs* (Black Virgins). The Chartres example was kept in the crypt of the building beside the 'holy well', at which it was found. The well was believed to have healing properties. Excavations in Chartres, in the general region of the cathedral, have revealed dozens of 'ritual' pits, of the kind which are now known to have had a wide distribution in Europe and are also found in Britain. The most dramatic of these is at the Roman fort of Newstead in the Scottish Lowlands, in the tribal territory of the Selgovae, 'the Hunters'. A striking landmark in the wild terrain are the three peaked hills which gave the fort its name, *Trimontium*. There can be little doubt that this was a pre-Roman cult centre of at least one, if not more of the local tribes. The contents of many of these pits have been published in some detail, in Ross and Feachem 1976, (230-7).

As we have seen, private and public matters were dealt with in assembly, as well as civil cases and miscellaneous legal matters. We must remember that the Druids, whose training lasted for up to twenty years and was completely oral, were skilled in many matters over and above religion and we know that they were also highly competent lawyers and expert healers such as could well be needed at these assemblies. The Celts had a reputation which was not unjustified, for being hot-tempered and not slow to seize weapons on the slightest pretext. As these assemblies were held in honour of the gods, it was deemed a heinous crime for anyone to break the peace which was an essential of such gatherings. Those who did so were in danger of losing their lives.

If Chartres was indeed the centre of all Gaul, it is likely that it was also a great focus of Druidism. At this festival, all the Druids

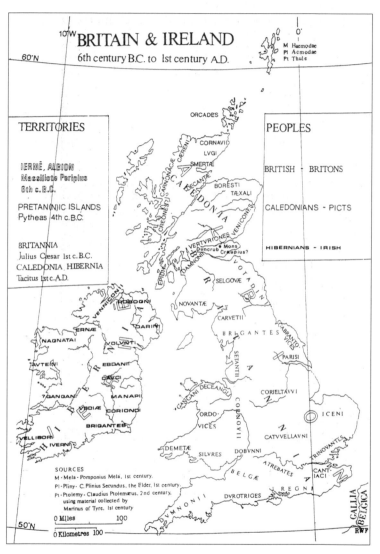

27 Some aspects of Britain and Ireland, sixth century BC – first century AD

met together in assembly. The Druidic system would seem to have been common to all the Celts. Caesar comments:

> These Druids, at a certain time of the year, meet within the borders of the Carnutes, whose territory is reckoned as the centre of all Gaul, and sit in conclave in a consecrated spot. Thither assemble from every side all that have disputes, and they obey the decisions and judgments of the Druids. It is believed their rule of life was discovered in *Britain* [my italics], and transferred thence to Gaul.

It is in fact from the British Isles *(27)*, and Ireland in particular, that the best evidence of such seasonal assemblies is to be found.

We know of another great festival or assembly celebrated on 1 August, at Lyon *(Lugudunum)* in honour of the god Lugus who gave his name to the site. After the Romanisation of Gaul the pagan feast was replaced by the celebration of the Emperor's birthday on the same date. In this way, the people were able to continue their ancient festivity while nominally worshipping the Emperor Augustus. Place-names suggest that there were many such August festivals throughout Gaul. In Ireland the August festival was likewise held in honour of the god Lugus and was known as *Lughnasa*. It is still vestigially celebrated down to the present time.

We may hazard a guess that the great national assembly referred to by Caesar is likely to have been held from 31 July, the time of Rivros (*Lughnasa* in Ireland), a time of fraughtness and fruition when the first fruits of the season were eaten and when the protection of the gods for the coming harvest was invoked. As all people connected with the land are aware, it is at this season that the burgeoning crops, which carry such promise of a rich harvest, can, in a very short time, be blighted by sudden storms and heavy rains.

A remarkable Gaulish calendar was found at Coligny, which is only a short distance from Lyon. This calendar demonstrates that a great feast was held in the month of *Rivros*, interpreted as 'great festal month'; and the thirteenth day of Rivros is described as 'great feast of the god', so the Lyon festival and the Irish feast, both in honour of Lugus, strongly suggest the pan-Celtic unity of the religion.

Certain places in Europe are, as their names indicate, associated with the god Lugus, e.g. Leidon, Loudun, Laon, to name but three. We may assume that the festival of Rivros *(Lughnasa)* was held in these places, and in any others which bear the god's name. Lugus was the equivalent of the classical Mercury. Our knowledge of his personality and history is best attested in Ireland. He is equated with the Welsh deity Lleu but because the literary tradition in Wales is somewhat later than that of Ireland, there does not seem to be any record of assemblies in his honour, but no doubt they originally occurred. This also can be applied to the city of Carlisle, the Roman name of which was *Luguvalium* ('strong in the god Lugus'), therefore presumably 'fortress of Lugus'. There are numerous traces of pagan Celtic religion in this region.

In Ireland, there are various legends which account for the origin of the Lughnasa festival. One of the most important of these is to be found in the ninth-century glossary entitled *Sanas Cormaic* (The Wisdom of Cormac), the original of which is in Irish. Bishop Cormac writes '*Lughnasa*, that is the *násadh* of Lugh, son of Ethle, i.e. an assembly held by him at the beginning of harvest each year at the coming of Lughnasa. *Násad* is a name for games or an assembly'. The assemblies at Tailtiu took place on Lughnasa, as did the assemblies at Carman. There are origin stories about most of the assemblies, and there are two accounts of the founding of the gathering called *Oenach Tailten*. One tells that it was established by Lugh to commemorate his foster-mother Tailtiu, who died there on the Calends of August. The other claims that he founded it in memory of both of his wives, Nás and Búi.

Lugh was undoubtedly the most mercurial character of the gods of Ireland known as the *Tuatha Dé Danann*, ('the People of the Goddess Danu'). In *Cath Maige Tuired* (the Battle of Moytura) the king Nuadu was holding a great feast at Tara for the *Tuatha*

Dé: 'Now there was a certain warrior on his way to Tara, whose name was Lug Samildánach ('The All-skilled') and there were two doorkeepers at Tara and the one on duty saw a strange company approaching with a fair and well-shaped young warrior, decked like a king, in the front of that company. They told the doorkeeper to announce their arrival at Tara. The doorkeeper asked 'Who is there?' 'Lug Lámfada (i.e. Lug of the long arm) is here. The doorkeeper asked Lug: 'What art do you practise? for no one without an art enters Tara'. 'Question me', he said, 'I am a wright.'. The doorkeeper answered: 'We do not need you: we have a wright already.' He then claimed to be a smith, a champion, a harper, a hero, a poet, an historian, a sorcerer. 'We do not need you. We have sorcerers *(corrguinigh)* already. Our Druids and our people of power are numerous'. Then Lug continued to recite all his remaining powers and skills, and to each one the doorkeeper replied 'We do not need you: we have one with each of those skills already,' and then Lug said: 'Ask the king whether he has a single man who possesses all these arts, and if he has, I will not enter Tara.' Then the doorkeeper went into the palace and told the king all that had happened. 'A warrior has come before the enclosure; his name is Samildánach, and all the arts which your household practise he himself is master of so he is the one of each and every art.' When that was related to Nuadu, the king, he said: 'Let him come into the enclosure; for never before has a man like him come to this fortress.' Then the doorkeeper let Lug pass him and he entered the fortress and sat down in the sage's seat, for he was a sage in every art.

The men of Ulster regularly held a great festival at Samain, Hallowe'en, 31 October, i.e. November Eve. A huge feast was made by the king, Conchobor, in Emain Macha. They kept the feast for three days before Samain, for three days after Samain, and on the day itself. It was one of the most important calendar festivals of the whole year, and still survives in the folk memory down to the present time. This period was devoted to sportive occupations: horse racing and other sports; feasting; drinking –

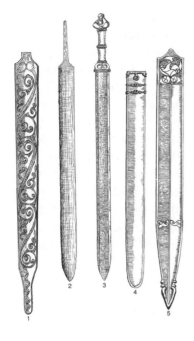

28 Examples of swords and scabbards:
1 Toome, Co Antrim, Northern Ireland
2 Late Iron Age Sword
3 Ribbed Sword with cast bronze Grip; Worton, Lancashire, England
4 Scabbard from the River Thames, London, England
5 Scabbard, Meare, Somerset, England

which often caused quarrels – and the recitation by each man present of his victories over powerful opponents. It was a time when the tricky gods mingled with men and the Otherworld was open so that mankind could enter at will. Each man had to give evidence of his bold deeds; this consisted in the production by the warriors of trophies, in the form of the tips of the tongues of their opponents (instead of carrying entire severed heads). They were brought in a special pouch or purse. There was some cheating by displaying the tongues of slain animals along with the human tongues. Each had to recite the details of his successes in combat. As they did so, they used to lay their long swords *(28)* across their thighs. They believed that demons inhabited their weapons and knew that should they depart from the truth their weapons would turn on them and slay them. It was a world fraught with hazard.

On one Samain, all the men of Ulster had assembled except
two of the most important warriors, Fergus mac Roich and
Conall Cearnach. The men of Ulster were impatient to get on
with the proceedings, but the chief hero, Cú Chulainn, avatar of
the god Lugh, objected because Fergus was his foster-father. A
fight seemed to be inevitable and Sencha, the wise man of the
Ulster people, moved in quickly to avert this disaster. He said 'Let
us, for the moment, play chess *(fidchell)*; let the Druid, and let the
jugglers perform.' And in this way the peace of the sacred feast
was ensured. (The Druids had the power to calm angry warriors
by their chanting and to occupy their minds with absorbing
games. The perpetual chanting of the Druids is referred to in
several texts, and this predilection for singing or monotonous
intoning persisted to within living memory in the Scottish
Gaelic tradition.)

The province of Ulster had been made into three partitions for
a year. A third part was given to Conchobor, the king, a third to
Cú Chulainn, his foster-son, and a third to Fintan, from *Dún Da-
Benn* (The Two-horned Fort). At the end of the year Conchobor
made the feast of Samain in Emain Macha. On that night the king
expected all the nobles of Ulster to partake in his feast but his
greatest warrior, Cú Chulainn was giving his *own* banquet for the
people of his territory in his fortress Dún Delgan. Conchobor
sent word to him to come to Emain Macha and Cú Chulainn said
he would not go, but his wife, the beautiful Emer, said that he
must go and speak with Conchobor who was his guardian. Loeg,
his charioteer, harnessed the horses and yoked the chariot. Cú
Chulainn put on his battle gear and leapt into his chariot and
came to Emain Macha. Sencha, the peacemaker, came out to meet
him and they talked together. Sencha was a skilled diplomat and
he had thought of a way in which he could preserve the peace
between Conchobor and Cú Chulainn. He succeeded and peace
was eventually made. They remained for three days and nights
drinking the banquet of Conchobor. The next year the warrior
Fintan had decided to prepare *his* banquet and there were a

hundred vats of every kind of ale in it and the feast was prepared
and ready. Cú Chulainn was the first to arrive at Emain. He had
just unyoked the horses when Fintan arrived. Fintan invited Cú
Chulainn to his banquet and, as usual, the wise Sencha resolved a
potentially dangerous situation by counselling the warriors to
spend the first half of the night with Fintan and the second half of
the night with Cú Chulainn. Both warriors agreed to this. So
messengers were sent to muster the people of the province of
Ulster to Fintan's banquet. They arrived at the festival assembly
and all the men of Ulster were present. There was lavish hospitality prepared, including entertainments, comfortable sleeping
places and provision of food and ale, 'so that the allowance of a
hundred of food and ale reached every nine of them'. It was then
that Cú Chulainn said to Loeg, his charioteer, 'Go out Loeg;
observe the stars, and estimate when the midnight comes.' When
midnight came, Loeg told Cú Chulainn. Cú Chulainn informed
Conchobor, who stood up with his bugle horn. The Ulster men
were silent when they saw the king was standing.

One of the tabus of the Ulster men was to speak before the
king; and one of the prohibitions of the king was to speak before
his Druids. The Druid Cathbad asked, 'What is it, Conchobor?' 'It
is time to go and drink Cú Chulainn's banquet,' replied the king.
The Ulster men went out upon the firm turf of the green. 'Good
Loeg,' said Cú Chulainn, 'start up the chariot, then speed up the
horses.' Cú Chulainn's horses broke into a furious, sudden start,
and the horses of the Ulster men followed suit. Then there began
a wild charge of chariots across country. Every hill was levelled,
every tree uprooted and the drunken warriors carried blindly on
towards their objective. But they were so intoxicated they took
the wrong route and were not in Ulster at all. The king said:
'Who will tell us what territory we are in?' None of them
answered, but Cú Chulainn said he would go and find out, so he
and Loeg separated from the rest and went on alone. After a
while, Cú Chulainn asked his charioteer what territory they
were in. 'I do not know,' said the charioteer, but Cú Chulainn

said 'I know', and proceeded to tell him where they were. Then heavy snow started and made it impossible to proceed. They returned to where they had left the Ulstermen. Sencha asked what territory they were in. 'We are' said Cú Chulainn, 'in the territory of Cú Roi mac Dairi.' 'Woe to us' said Sencha. 'Don't say that' said Cú Chulainn, 'for I will give guidance to the Ulstermen in the same way.' Conchobor said: 'Where shall we camp this night?' 'On the fair green of Senchlochar' said Cú Chulainn, 'and Tara Luachra is near'. (Tara Luachra is in the south-west of Ireland – Ulster is in the north!)

Unfortunately for the Ulstermen, there was a great feast at Tara Luachra that night, and Ailill and Medb, king and queen of Connacht, had come accompanied by their chieftains, to drink to celebrate the birth of Medb's son. There was a great gathering. Medb was a warrior-queen and she had two of her Druids on guard. Their names were Crom Deroil and Crom Darail, the two foster-sons of the famous Druid Cathbad. They were on the wall of Tara keeping guard, when Crom Deroil said: 'Have you seen what I have seen?' 'What thing?' said Crom Darail. 'It seems to me that I can see swords of crimson warfare, and that I can hear the tread of multitudes coming towards us from the east.' Crom Deroil replied 'That is no army but the huge oak trees we passed yesterday.' 'If so', said the other, 'why have they got the great royal chariots under them?' 'They are not chariots,' said the other 'but the royal fortresses past which we came'. And so the conversation continued. The warrior Cú Roi heard the two Druids quarrelling on the walls of Tara Luachra. Then the sun rose and Crom Deroil said to the other Druid, 'Now we can see the host'. The host advanced with such a fury that all the spears fell from their racks, the shields from their hooks, and the swords in the armoury all fell to the ground. The coming of the host was terrible. The two Druids fell in fits and faintings. Crom Derail fell over the wall outside and Crom Darail fell over the wall inside. Even so, Crom Deroil got up and looked at the first band that came into the green. So great was the host of the Ulster warriors that the snow dissolved and melted 30ft on either side of them. Crom Deroil said, 'I see a barbaric host and I do not know whether they are Irishmen or foreigners, but if they are Irishmen, they are Ulster men.' The host arrived and the Druids described it to the queen, Medb. She and her court identified each band in turn.

Next came a trio clothed as warriors. Two of them were young; the third had a forked beard. Not one of the great host saw them, but *they* could see the whole host. They were in fact three young gods of the Tuatha Dé Danann who had mingled with the host to incite it to battle. Then Crom Deroil described a large-thighed, noble, immensely tall man with a splendid grey garment about him, and at either side of him were nine men. In his hand was a terrible iron staff, which had a rough end and a smooth end. His game consisted in laying the rough end on the heads of the nine, whom he would kill in the space of a moment. He would then lay the smooth end on them, so that he would bring them to life again. 'That is a wonderful description', said the queen, 'who then is he?' 'Not hard to tell', said Cú Roi, 'the great Dagda, son of Ethliu, the good god of the Tuatha Dé Danann, and no one in the host sees him'. *He* was the God of Druidism.

The four calendar festivals of the ancient Celtic year are still celebrated vestigially in the British Isles today. The stories about them are extremely numerous and convey a wonderful impression of the superstitious nature of the early Celts, a characteristic which is fully attested in history by the classical writers and others. Glimpses of the Otherworld of the gods are mingled with humorous episodes and long descriptions of the harsh reality of life in early Ireland as it was seen through the eyes of the brilliant story-tellers, who played such an important rôle in preserving the ancient traditions, which are still recounted in some form by present-day *seanachaidhean* (story-tellers).

As we have seen, the feast of Lughnasa was inaugurated by the pan-Celtic god Lugus, the Mercury of the pagan Celts. His Irish name, the *Ildánach* ('the many-skilled') testifies to the Irish belief in his unique powers and the legends about him are legion. As horse racing was a regular feature of the Lughnasa festival, it is worth noting that this god was accredited with its invention. There is an episode in one of the *Dindshenchas* stories which is difficult to understand. In this tradition, Lug drowns his horses in a loch. The reason for this is not given but it may be connected with the fact that riding horses across water was a regular sport at the later Lughnasa gatherings. The festival must have been widespread throughout the British Isles and in Europe. One of the finest stories comes from Cornwall and there are many tales of the ancient gatherings in Scotland, as well as traces of them in England and Wales. The Celtic culture was rooted in the *land*, which was from earliest times venerated by the people and regarded as being under the protection of some powerful goddess *(plate 8)* who remained guardian of the land while the male gods moved when circumstances brought about tribal expansion or movement of any kind.

There was a deep feeling that stemmed from the Druids, that moral wrong, especially when committed by the king and others of high office, would damage not only the tribe, but the total fertility of the land itself. Crops would fail, fish would disappear from estuaries and rivers, cattle would be smitten by disease, and even the bees would be less prolific in the production of the all-important honey, on which the sacred drink *mead* was based. As so many of the festivals were initiated with the well-being of the land, and therefore of the tribe, in mind, it is not surprising that those whose lives consisted in the hard labour of working that land, and caring for its stock and produce, continued to hold these festivals dear, and to keep them alive in some places and in some form, down to the present day.

The Celtic year, as we have seen, was divided into four quarters and each quarter was marked by a festival which was regarded as essential for the well-being of the coming months. There were two Irish words for festival: *Oenach* and *féis*; the Welsh word is *gwyl*.

Samain (or *Samhain*) (31 October – 1 November) was regarded as the Celtic New Year. It was the most dark and portenteous of the four festivals: a time when the Otherworld was believed to be open and accessible to human beings, and when the gods entered the world of men and were dangerous. They often wrought apparent havoc which was later discovered to have been but an illusion created by these tricky Otherworld beings. The Celts did not *love* their gods, but realised the vital importance of propitiation and thus this was a night when prolific sacrifices were offered to them. There are numerous Old Irish tales which describe the horrors of Samain and it is the festival which has perhaps survived longest. It is still celebrated with great bonfires – all four festivals were fire festivals, but Samain had the greatest conflagrations. It was a night when glimpses of the future could be had by carrying out various rites.

Of great significance is the fact that the Samain Assembly took place at Tara, the seat of the kings of Ireland, and there is certainly evidence that human sacrifice was carried out as well as the offering of animals. The assemblies at Tlachtga in modern Co. Meath also took place at Samain.

The second festival of the Celtic calendar year was anciently known as *Imbolc* or *Óimelc*. It was held on the eve of 1 February, and on February Day. St Brigit, in the Hebrides, was believed to be the foster-mother of Christ, and her feast-day coincided with the Purification of the Virgin, so paganism and Christianity were neatly brought together. The night before the first, and the day following, were highly portentous times. In the Hebrides the festival was known as *Lá Féil Bhride*. In Ireland, it was known as St. Brigit's Day and generally it was regarded as the first day of Spring, and so of the farmer's year. The farmers hoped for good weather to hasten the Spring ploughing and the fishermen prayed for calm seas to start their work. On every St Brigit's Eve, all the farmers' wives in Ireland used to make a cake which was eaten accompanied by ale and music and general festivity. Like the Hebrideans, it was believed that the saint journeyed about the countryside herself on the Eve of her festival, blessing her people and their livestock. A cake or pieces of bread and butter were placed outside on the window-sill and a sheaf of corn put beside it to refresh the saint's white cow which accompanied her. In Ireland, the most characteristic custom was the making of the *crois Bríde* (the St Brigit's cross) which was often hung up in the house and in the byre as well, to gain her protection. Crosses were made of rushes and in some places of straw *(plate 25)*.

There were many variants to the Brigit traditions, some very elaborate charms, spells and customs which were clearly of ultimate pagan origin. This festival, which was celebrated so elaborately, stems not only from an ancient calendar festival that has been taken over into Christianity, but Bride was ultimately a pagan goddess who became a Christian saint, as was so often the case. She was frequently envisaged like so many Celtic deities, in threefold form (e.g. she was one of three infants born at the same birth and having the same name, her father being the great Dagda ('Good God'), the Irish god of Druidism. The number three, as we have seen, was the most important number for the Celtic people, and gods and goddesses are frequently portrayed in Celtic iconography in Europe and the British Isles as three separate individuals; the sanctity of this number is further attested by the fact that many horned animals are represented as having three horns *(10* and *plate 15)*. Although St Patrick is alleged to have banished the serpents from Ireland, Brigit is very clearly associated with this creature in the Hebrides, and it was believed by the people that, on the sacred day, 1 February, the serpent would come from its hole in the hills and a propitiatory hymn was sung to it. There are several versions of this invocation, for example:

> Early on Bride's morn
> The serpent shall come from the hole,
> I will not molest the serpent,
> Nor will the serpent molest me.

Another version says:

> On the feast day of Bride
> The head will come off the caiteanach(?)
> The daughter of Ivor will come from the knoll
> With tuneful whistling.
>
> The serpent will come from the hole
> On the brown day of Bride
> Though there should be three feet of snow
> On the flat surface of the ground.

Although it is recorded that there were no snakes in Ireland, early Irish mythology has many references to snakes and serpentiform monsters. As the collector of this marvellous material, Alexander Carmichael, correctly surmises: 'This hymn in connection with the saint-goddess Bride indicates vestigial serpent-worship.'

The Isle of Man, which until the middle of the twentieth century, spoke a form of Gaelic called Manx, has its own rich folklore and many traditions about this saint. *Laa'l Breeshey* ('Brigit's feast-day'), was observed. As in the Hebrides domestic preparations were made to welcome the saint in the hope that she would stay the night in people's households.

Beltain

Beltain – 1 May – was one of the most ancient calendar festivals in the Celtic year, sacred to the pan-Celtic god Belenos, who was venerated from Italy across Europe and throughout the British Isles. The mythological Welsh king *Beli Mawr* is in all probability a folk memory of this great god who was equivalent to the classical Apollo and a suitable deity to preside over this fertile season, celebrated by great bonfires all over Europe, and never, seemingly, likened to any Christian saint. It was a period of great rejoicing. In Man it was known as *Laa-Boaldyn*, 'the Beltain', as it was called in Irish. Cormac, in his ninth-century Irish glossary, says the name arose from two fires, 'which the Druids of Ireland used to make with great incantations'. And he adds that the Druids used to drive the cattle between two fires in order to protect them against diseases. It was the first day of summer and various plants and branches of flowering shrubs and trees were strewn inside and outside people's houses. These were nearly always yellow flowers in Ireland, and were gathered before dark on May Day Eve. This custom still persists in many places. Some people decked their horses' bridles with flowers, and there were many May Day festivals. Wells particularly were visited, and again decked with flowers, and it was everywhere a day for lovers and sexual licence. In Gaelic it was known as *Latha Buidhe Bealtain* ('the yellow day of Beltain'). Sacrifices used to be offered for the preservation of the cattle, and processions made round the fields, holding burning torches of wood, in order to obtain a blessing for the growing crops, were also commonly carried out. It was a day of great sacrifices, a day when all fires were extinguished, so that they could be rekindled from the flames of one special, sacred bonfire. It would seem to have been a day when human sacrifices were carried out, and there are still traces of this in Gaelic folklore, as in other contexts. A special cake or bannock used to be made on a griddle, and it was believed that a portion of it was deliberately blackened by some supernatural agent. This is described in the Glenlyon ritual (q.v.).

May Day was celebrated throughout Europe with similar festivities, and it was the only festival that was not Christianised by association with a particular saint. There are many tales of this festival pertaining to the ancient Celtic world. It was a time of sacrifice and propitiation, as well as of celebration and fertility. The maypole was the focal point of the festivities.

In Wales the first day of May was known as *Calan Mai* and at an earlier time, *Calan Haf* ('the Calends of Summer'). It was a day when farm servants were hired, hiring fairs were held, and the people gathered in the evening to dance round the maypole, as elsewhere, and to indulge in sports and other pastimes.

All these seasonal festivals were, of course, in pagan times under the aegis of the Druids and the gods, and were too deeply rooted in the Celtic mind for them ever to yield entirely to Christian hostility. Eventually, once paganism ceased to be a forceful power in society, a compromise was reached, and thus they have survived in some form or another, down to the present time.

Chapter 8

UNITY AND DIVERSITY

Druids and the early Church

Rather than attempting to cover this lengthy and complex subject in detail, I have thought it preferable to make a selection from the copious and diverse source-material which exists.

In the chronicles dealing with early Christian Ireland, the Druids are frequently mentioned. The Tripartite Life of Patrick contains three semi-historical homilies on the saint. The document dates from the tenth century at the latest and, as usual embodies traditions of a much earlier age. In the seventeenth century the Franciscan scholar Colgan owned three very ancient copies of this work. These have now been lost. The oldest surviving manuscript is in the British Museum and dates to the fourteenth–fifteenth century. In this ancient history of St Patrick it is related that the saint came to Ireland in the fifth year of the reign of 'a certain fierce heathen king' Loegaire, son of Niall, who had a royal residence at Tara. He had at his court Druids of whom the chief were named Lochru and Lucatmael. They foretold that 'an evil-lawed prophet would come hither over sea to their land ... and that he would cast the kings and lords out of their realm, and would destroy all the images of the idols.' Seeing in vision the tonsured head of this interloper, they nicknamed him 'adzehead'.

Adzehead will come over a furious sea
His mantle head-holed, his staff crook-headed.
Adzehead will come who will build cities,
Who will consecrate churches, pinnacles music –
Many conical caps (of belfries), a realm round croziers houses.

The king, accompanied by his Druids goes forth with the intention
of killing Patrick. However, the Druid Lochru is raised up in the air
through the prayers of the saint and dashed down. Lucatmael, the
second Druid tries to poison the saint and brings darkness over the
whole land. Patrick challenges the Druid to a contest of powers. So
a hut is built and into this goes the Druid wearing the saint's chasuble; Benén, Patrick's disciple goes in wearing the tunic of the
Druid. The hut is then ignited. Benén escapes unhurt, but the
Druid's tunic is destroyed by the flames; the Druid dies, but the
Saint's chasuble remains undamaged by the fire. This remarkable
event is described in similar words in another ancient homily on St
Patrick, contained in the *Lebor Brecc* (The Speckled Book).

There is also the famous story of how Patrick decided to celebrate Easter-tide at Tara, seat of the kings of Ireland, 'the chief
abode of the idolatry and Druidism of Ireland'. Loegaire, with the
other kings and leaders, had come to celebrate the 'the high-tide of
the heathen, namely, the feast of Tara'. At the command of the
king's Druids, all the fires were extinguished, and it was forbidden,
under the pain of death, to kindle any fire before the pagan fire was
lit on the hill of Tara. However, Patrick 'struck the pascal fire' at
Ferta Fer Feice, 'The Graves of Fiace's Men' near Slane. The Druids
then warned the king that 'unless it is quenched on the night on
which it was made it will not be quenched till Doomsday'.

Patrick and the Druids

Loegaire, son of Niall of the Nine Hostages *(Niall 'Naoi-ghiallach)*,
became King of Ireland in AD 428. Four years after his accession he

came face to face with St Patrick who had returned to Ireland where, as a boy named Succet, he had many years previously been held as a slave, having been captured by Irish marauders in Britain, his native country. Loegaire was a powerful pagan ruler; Patrick was now an evangelising Christian whom God had 'called' back to his place of enslavement in order to Christianise his former captors. The Druids contended with him; Patrick prayed against 'the spells of women, smiths and Druids'. Goibniu (the smith) had a reputation for magic even amongst Christians. A spell for making butter in an eighth-century manuscript, preserved in St Gall appeals to his 'science'. Idols are mentioned frequently. Gildas also speaks of 'images mouldering away within and without the deserted temples, with stiff and deformed features', forsaken shrines of forgotten gods.

In the Celtic Lives of the Saints, and perhaps most particularly those of the Irish churchmen and women, are embedded what would seem to be some of the most archaic and genuine examples of pre-Christian custom and belief. In all the Celtic countries there were numerous Celtic divinities, male and female who survived in the rôle of guardians of sacred wells, and special places – the *genii locii* of post-Christian veneration. Like the gods themselves, these may be envisaged as having bird or animal form, or a triple persona; or they could lurk in the boughs and branches of some sacred pagan tree, many of which must have reached a great age.

Adamnán, who was ninth Abbott of Iona, gives an extremely early and surely genuine account. A detailed map in the front of his *Life of Columba* shows a site named *Cladh nan Druineach* or *Druidhnee* ('Cemetery of the Druids') *(18)*. This suggests several important questions. Who, for example, were the Druids who were buried in the cemetery on Iona? They must obviously have antedated the Christian settlement on the island and it would not be surprising, in view of the Greek Demetrius' comments about 'holy men' occupying islands round the coast of Britain, to find that there was a Druidic presence there at some period in the past. Were the Druids then Pictish Druids? And had they abandoned the shores of Iona long before Columba's establishment of the monastery there? Demetrius then remarked on the numerous small islands round the coast of Britain which were inhabited by 'holy men' (or gods perhaps) and the effect on the air round about when any of the 'great ones' died.

Columba's miracles

Like the Druids themselves, Columba was a healer. He also had the power to expel from Iona the great hosts of malevolent spirits which inhabited it. He calmed the turbulent waves by means of prayer and reached his destination in safety. When returning from the country of the Picts, where he had been for some ten days in his mission of conversion, Columba hoisted his sail when the wind was against him and made as rapid a voyage as if the wind had been favourable, to the astonishment of the Druids. On other occasions, contrary winds were by his prayers made fair. Likewise, in the land of the Picts, he took a white stone from the river, blessed it in order that it should work certain cures; and that stone, contrary to nature, floated like an apple when placed in water. This divine miracle was carried out in the presence of King Brude and his household (Reeves 1988).

In the same country he performed an even greater miracle, by raising to life the dead child of a humble believer, and restoring him to his father and mother. At another time, when the blessed man was still a young deacon in Hibernia, residing with the holy bishop, Findbarr, the supply of wine required for the sacred mysteries ran out, and he changed by his prayer pure water into good wine. An immense blaze of heavenly light was on many occasions seen by some of the brethren surrounding him in the light of day, as well as in the dark night. Columba had great gifts of prophecy. Prophecy was also one of the most renowned powers of the Druids.

THE THREEFOLD DEATH

In Adamnán's *Life of Saint Columba* we have perhaps the earliest reference to the Celtic motif of the triple death: Columba prophesies that Aedh Dubh will die three deaths: he will be pierced in the neck by a spear; he will fall from a tree; he will be drowned. This is a very ancient motif and is Indo-European in origin. Traces of it still survive in folklore (see Ross, 1986).

Columba had a remarkably fine and powerful singing voice. Once when they were near the fortress of King Brude, near Inverness, the saint was chanting the evening hymns with some of the brethren, as usual, outside the king's fortifications; some Druids approached them and did all they could to prevent God's praises being sung in the midst of a pagan nation. When Columba saw this, he began to sing the 44th Psalm, and at the same moment, 'so wonderfully loud, like pealing thunder, did his voice become, that king and people were struck with terror and amazement'.

COLUMBA AND THE CRANE

In Adamnán's account, Columba called one of the brothers to him one morning and told him to sit down and wait on the western shore of the island (Hy) for a crane, a stranger from the northern region of Hibernia 'and hath been driven about by the various winds, shall come, weary and fatigued, after the ninth hour, and lie down before thee on the beach quite exhausted. Treat that bird tenderly, take it to some neighbouring house, where it may be kindly received and carefully nursed and fed by thee for three days and three nights. When the crane is refreshed with the three days' rest, and is unwilling to abide any longer with us, it shall fly back with renewed strength to the pleasant part of Scotia (Ireland) from which it originally hath come. This bird do I consign to thee with such special care because it cometh from our own native place.' The brother obeyed, and on the third day, after the ninth hour, he watched as he was bid for the arrival of the expected guest. As soon as the crane came and alighted on the shore, he took it up gently and carried it to a dwelling that was near, where in its hunger he fed it. On his return to the monastery in the evening, the saint, without any questions, said to him, 'God bless thee, my child, for thy kind attention to this foreign visitor, that shall not remain long on its journey but shall return within three days to its old home.' As the saint predicted, so exactly did the event prove, for after being nursed carefully for three days, the bird then gently rose on its wings to a great height in the sight of the hospitable man, and marking for a little its path through the air homewards, it directed its course across the sea to Hibernia, straight as it could fly, on a calm day.

Next follows an account of Columba's many miracles. A youth fell into the *Boand* (Boyne) and was drowned. He was 20 days under the water. He had a number of books with him in a leather satchel and they too fell into the river. When the body was recovered and the satchel opened it was found that all the books were quite dry and unharmed. This was because one of the volumes had been written by Columba himself and it was as safe and dry as if it had been in a desk. It was widely believed that no injury could come to any books written by St Columba if they should chance to be immersed in water. The same applied to fire which was powerless to harm Columba's books.

When Columba was in Pictland he learnt of a well worshipped by the Picts as a god. This well was inhabited by an evil spirit and men believed in it and worshipped it. The saint went fearlessly to the spring. The Druids, whom he had often sent away from him, vanquished, and confounded, were delighted by this, thinking Columba would suffer like others 'from the touch of that baleful water', but the saint, first having washed his hands and invoked the name of Christ, drank of the water which he had blessed. And from that day on the demons departed from the water. Not only was it forbidden to do harm to anyone, but it now cured many diseases from which the people suffered.

Once he was at sea and a great storm blew up and the sailors were terrified. Columba stood at the prow, stretched up his hands to heaven and the storm immediately abated. His companions were amazed and praised the Lord.

THE TAKING OF MILK FROM A BULL

When the saint was staying in the house of a rich man, two men came to him; one of them was a sorcerer. The sorcerer took milk from a bull, on the request of the saint; he then commanded the full vessel to be given to him and he blessed it and it turned into blood. The bull, which was dying as a result of this sorcery was sprinkled with water that had been blessed by the saint and rapidly recovered. Animal miracles are very frequent in the legends of Columba. There was a noble man in exile amongst the Picts called Tarain. He was treacherously put to death by a man whom the saint had appointed to care for him. Columba cursed him and a horrid death befell him.

LOCH NESS MONSTER

This is the earliest account of the monster that still intrigues us and whose existence never seems to be capable of proof or disproof.

Columba was staying in the province of the Picts when he had occasion to cross the river *Nesa* (Ness). When he reached the bank of the river, he saw some of the inhabitants burying an unfortunate man who seemingly, a short time before was seized by the monster as he was swimming and badly mauled. His body was recovered from the water by a hook. Columba ordered one of his companions to swim across and bring back the boat that was moored there. He obeyed at once. But the monster, so far from being satisfied, was only eager for more prey. It was lying at the bottom of the stream, and when it felt the water disturbed above by the man swimming, it suddenly rushed out, and, giving an awful roar darted after him, with its mouth wide open. Then Columba, observing this, raised his holy hand, while all the rest, brethren as well as strangers, were overcome with terror. Invoking the name of God, he made the sign of the cross in the air and commanded the monster, saying: 'Thou shalt go no further, nor touch the man; go back with all speed.' At the voice of the saint the monster was terrified, and fled. Then the brethren, seeing that the monster had gone back, and their comrade was saved, were struck with amazement and praised God. Even the barbarous heathens, who were present, were forced by the greatness of this miracle, which they themselves had seen, to magnify the God of the Christians.

Columba blessed Iona *(Hy)* and banished the serpents and reptiles from the island. Columba clearly had the gift of miracles which the Druids themselves claimed to possess, as did the prophets of the Old Testament.

COLUMBA OVERCOMES BROICHAN

One day Broichan asked Columba on what day he proposed to sail. The saint replied: 'in three days, God willing'. Broichan replied; 'On the contrary thou shalt not be able for I can make the winds unfavourable to the voyage and cause a great darkness to envelop you in its shade.' So the same day Columba, with a large number of his followers went to Loch Ness. It had grown very dark and the wind was very violent and contrary. The Druids had power to raise storms, but the power of prayer was greater. Calling upon Christ, Columba embarked in his small boat; his sailors hesitated when he ordered them to raise the sails. No sooner had this been done than the vessel ran against the wind at an extraordinary speed while a great crowd looked on. And after a short time, the wind, which had been against them, veered round to help them on their voyage 'to the intense astonishment of all the onlookers, and the holy man reached land in safety'.

The Lives of the Celtic Saints in general are an excellent source for details of paganism and pre-Christian practices. There are some dramatic examples of encounters and contests between pagan and priest in the remarkable and archaic traditions of Ireland; only a few of these may be considered, however, for the depth and breadth of

29 Wooden figure from well
at Montbuoy, Loiret, France

the subject cannot allow of too much space being given to any one aspect of Druidic practice and belief. Columba's Life is of singular importance in that it introduces us to the Druids of Pictland. Ireland is the most valuable source, but its very prolific nature means that only a small part of the total evidence can be looked at here.

Genealogies of the saints and prayers for protection from evil pagan forces

THE GENEALOGY OF BRIDE (SLOINNTIREACHD BHRIDE)

The genealogy of the holy maiden Bride
Radiant flame of gold, noble foster-mother of Christ.
Bride the daughter of Dughaill Duinn,
Son of Aodh, son of Art, son of Conn,
Son of Crearar, son of Cis, son of Carmac son of Carruin.

Every day and every night
That I say the genealogy of Bride,
I shall not be killed, I shall not be harried,
I shall not be imprisoned, I shall not be wounded,
Neither shall Christ leave me in forgetfulness.

'No fire, no sun, no moon shall burn me,
No lake, no water, nor sea shall drown me
No arrow of fairy nor dart of elf shall wound me,
And I under the protection of my Holy Mary,
And my gentle foster-mother is my beloved Bride.

This prayer for protection has been preserved in the Outer Hebrides perhaps for hundreds of years in the oral tradition of a people who not only held their past in high esteem, but had found an acceptable way of equating the dictates of the new faith of Christianity with the age-old spells and incantations of indubitably pagan origin. Here, the goddess *Brigit*, a Celtic *Minerva* in some of her many aspects, has been equated with the gentle saint *Bride*, who was reared in the household of a Druid in Ireland in the fifth century AD. She was much concerned with cattle and dairy products in the folk memories of the Hebrides to within living memory. She visited every house on her feast day, *Imbolc*, 1 February, the time of the purification of the Virgin in the temple. She was followed by her white cow, and gifts were laid out for her in the form of food for herself and her faithful companion. She was regarded as the foster-child of the Virgin, and in this way both pagan and Christian traditions could be tactfully amalgamated and the old faith preserved under the aegis of the Church.

Genealogy was an important aspect of the entire Celtic tradition at all periods; it was accredited with a power of safe-guarding the one who recited it. On the contrary, the concept of the threefold death was known and feared in a very much earlier Celtic world and persisted down the long ages in spite of change and Christian precept. We meet the threefold death again in another impassioned plea for divine protection from evil. This example of the dark fears which beset the Christian soul in a pagan milieu takes us back to the period of the early church and to St Brigit, who is alleged to have made St Patrick's winding-sheet. Like Brigit, Patrick had come to Ireland as a slave when a youth, from a prosperous British family background. Brigit was born in Ireland where her mother, likewise of good breeding had been brought in slavery. Patrick finally escaped on a ship bound for Gaul and eventually managed to return to his family. Many years later he was called by God to return to the place of his enslavement, and to bring Christianity to those people who still lived in ignorance of the true faith. It was a brave step for the former slave to take; and his famous 'prayer for protection' shows even more clearly than does that of Brigit in the latter day Hebrides, the power and terror of the forces threatening his mission. This ancient prayer, or Breastplate (Latin *lorica*, Gaelic *luireach*) is still sometimes sung as a hymn in churches, and is deeply moving. The text is of considerable length and I have selected those lines which seem directly relevant to our subject:

ST PATRICK'S BREASTPLATE

At Temur (Tara) today I invoke the mighty power of the Trinity. I believe in the Trinity under the Unity of the God of the Elements. ...

... At Temur today (I place) the strength of heaven, the light of the sun, the whiteness of snow, the force of fire, the rapidity of lightning, the swiftness of the wind, the depth of the sea, the stability of the earth, the hardness of rocks (between me and the powers of paganism and demons). ...

... I place all those powers between me and every evil unmerciful power directed against my soul and my body, (as a protection) against the incantations of false prophets (*saibfhatha*), against the black laws of Gentilism (*dubhrechtu Gentliuchta*), against the false laws of heresy (*Saibrechtu heretecta*), against the treachery of idolatry (*himcellacht n-idlachta*), against the spells of women (*brichta ban*), smiths (*goband*), and Druids (*druad*), against every knowledge (*fiss*) which blinds the soul of man.

May Christ today protect me against *poisons* (*neim*), against *burning* (*losgad*), against *drowning* (*badud*), against *wounding* (*guin*), until I deserve much reward.

The Breastplate ends with a number of 'bindings', a very interesting Celtic concept which may be compared with the numerous oaths taken on some supernatural or natural force. These words, or variants of them are still sung at the present time:

> I bind unto myself today
> The power of God to hold and lead
> His eye to watch, his might to stay
> His ear to harken to my need;
> The wisdom of my God to teach
> His hand to guide, his shield to ward;
> The word of God to give me speed
> His heavenly host to be my guard.

This evocation of human fragility and pagan forces makes a powerful impact on the listener, conjuring up vivid images of the vulnerability of the Christian soul when faced with the mantic, destructive powers of Druids, and the force of faith in Christ, and the unseen but trusted ability of the Creator to shield and save. But, as we shall see, paganism was not only a dark religion in the Celtic lands; there was much of beauty and brightness to offset the powers of hostility and sacrifice.

In this passionate invocation for protection against all the dark horrors of the natural and the spiritual world of paganism, we once again have a clear reference to the ancient trinitarian concept of the Threefold Death. Here the death mentioned is by burning, drowning, and wounding, the three types of death suffered, for example, by Diarmaid mac Cearbhall, king of Tara in the sixth century, and possibly still an adherent of the old Druidic faith. His death occurred at Samain, Hallowe'en, a time of terror and superstitious rites, including, it would seem, sacrifice. The gods mingled with mankind, and the Otherworld in which they resided was capable of entry by mankind – at their peril. Threefold deaths were as a rule prophesied, usually by a seer or Druid. Diarmaid asks his Druids to divulge what the nature of his death is to be. They prophesy that he will die by means of a weapon, and the king thinks that can be easily avoided. Next they foresee that he will drown in a vat of ale. Finally they prophesy that his death will come about by burning. Diarmaid rejects their prophecy with scorn. However, on the night of Samain the Druidic prophecy of a triple death is fulfilled. The king of Tara is wounded by a spear, the feasting hall is set on fire and, in order to escape the encompassing flames, Diarmaid leaps into the great vat of ale and so drowns. Another king of Tara, a cousin of Diarmaid's, Muircheartach mac Erca, king of Tara, meets with an identical death at Samain. It is this dread and pagan fate from which the good saint seeks protection – as does his gentle contemporary, Bride, or Brigit, according to the tradition, centuries later. Patrick, Benén (Saint Benignus), and Brigit themselves form a trio of saints who were most venerated and loved in the fifth and early sixth centuries.

The changing world of the Druids

The Christianisation of Ireland was a gradual process and the Druids, in some guise or another, survived. 'Druidism' with its connotations of magical powers and heathenish practices came under strong censure from the 'Men of God' – many of whom stemmed from a pagan background themselves. We have to remember that the early Celtic church was created or supported by those whose origins were *Celtic*, who spoke Irish Gaelic and whose immediate ancestors had lived under the strict and exclusive rule of pagan kings and their Druids. The Celts did not exist in an isolated world. They travelled widely in Europe, where they met fellow scholars and men of learning from as far afield as Greece, Italy, possibly Galatia, Iberia, and the island of Britain. News of the birth of the Saviour would certainly have reached them at an early period. In one fictitious Irish story the king, Conchobor mac Nessa, is recorded as having died of grief upon hearing of the crucifixion of Christ. The Celts studied Greek and spoke and wrote in that language. The fact that Christ was the son of God, who came to earth to save mankind, that he was a teacher and a preacher, a healer, a great prophet and finally, an innocent victim of sacrifice, would inevitably have a strong appeal for the learned classes of the wider Celtic world, especially the Druids. Christianity, however, constituted a clear and potent threat to the continuing *official* practice of Druidism. The Druids, whose supreme authority had gone unchallenged in their tribal society, were now faced with a difficult choice. Some undoubtedly went into the Church and embraced Christianity. Others became scholars and worked in the *scriptoria* on manuscripts and their illumination. Their rôle as poets was an enduring one, and they committed to writing the old stories as we have seen, no doubt with a great deal of expurgation.

Samson was a fifth-century saint of Welsh provenance, but his *Vita* was written in Brittany, perhaps in the first quarter of the seventh century. He was believed to have been chosen by God,

30 Cernunnos with Ram-Horned Serpent.
Aquae Nerii, Néris-les-Bains, Allier, France

which gave him a sanctity unparalleled in the age in which he was
to live. His mother had been barren until, in a dream, she was told
of the coming of a son who would be a man of God. The child, a
boy named Samson, was to become a disciple of the renowned
Abbot Illtud. Apart from the *Vita's* clear Biblical associations, it is
obvious that the hagiographer was influenced by 'pagan Celtic
religious iconography and themes'. Thus we are told that Illtud,
with whom Samson studied, was a learned magician (i.e. Druid) by
birth and was gifted with second sight. The use of the term *magicus*
is reminiscent enough of the Druidic world for a number of
scribes to 'correct' it to *magnificus*. Samson kills a snake and tames a
witch who brandishes a bloody trident. 'Following his ordination
as bishop, fire comes from his mouth and nostrils' (See further
Ross, 1967 & 1992).

The snake plays an important rôle in pagan Celtic cults. Macha,
one of the three war goddesses who could assume various forms,
especially the crow or raven, appeared as a vicious serpent which
twisted itself round the legs of the hero Cú Chulainn when he was
fighting in single combat with his Connacht enemy in her bid to
destroy him. The reason for her enmity was that he had refused her
sexual advances.

In Celtic mythology, the serpent was frequently portrayed in the
iconography as having ram-horns or a horned ram's head. It is
particularly associated with the stag-god Cernunnos 'the Horned'
(30) and with the cult of healing waters. St Brigit, who lived at the
beginning of the seventh century, in many ways resembles the
Goddess Sul of Aquae Sulis (Bath) and had, like her, a perpetually
blazing fire which was never allowed to be extinguished and was
guarded by nine virgins in her foundation at Kildare *(Cill Dara)*.
No man was allowed to enter the sanctuary. There are many early
Celtic tales in which fire plays an important rôle. The Druids,
according to the classics, believed that the world would never end
but that, from time to time, fire or water would prevail. There are
many examples in Celtic mythology of deities, demons and
animals which breathe forth fire. The Druids believed that they

could control the elements and indeed claimed to have created the world. They were also capable of transforming others and themselves. In one version of the Cattle Raid of Cúailnge they are described as wandering about amongst the stones in the form of deer.

Summary

The spirit of the Druids remained as an essential element in the new faith and the Christianisation of the Celtic world. It was not, however, their darker, pagan powers that persisted, but their learning and education, their rôle as teachers, as poets and prophets. The word 'Druid' was heavily expurgated from the textual material, but the Druids were never quite banished from Celtic society. They were highly learned, and had thus much to contribute to the rich intellectual heritage of Ireland. In Wales, likewise, the names *Derwydd*, and *Dryw*, tended to disappear, but their powers of poetry and prophecy remained. In the medieval Welsh poem *Armes Prydein*, ('the Prophecy of Britain') from the Book of Taliesin, (Williams & Bromwich, 1972 12,13) we learn *'Dysgogan derwydon meint a derwyd'* ('Druids foretell all that will happen'). Thus it is, in their enduring rôle as prophets and poets, that the Druids have achieved a lasting and acceptable position in the Welsh, as in the Irish, tradition.

— Chapter 9 —
FOLKLORE AND FESTIVAL

Some areas of the Scottish Highlands would seem to have preserved their pre-Christian, or pagan customs and beliefs to a greater extent than others. There are many factors which have dictated such survivals and non-survivals. Perhaps one of the most important of these is the degree of isolation that any given area retained in a changing world where the old ways were replaced by the new, and tradition was despised by the young. Central Perthshire is an area that kept alive a rich store of archaic customs and beliefs, tales and legends, until the Second World War brought about the breakdown of such practices in a way that the first had failed completely to eradicate. Two very strange and ancient practices, which in an earlier Celtic world would have been very much under the authority of the Druids, still survived in an aetiolated form until the middle of the twentieth century at least, although their true significance had undoubtedly been lost.

Both are centred in the wild, remote and beautiful mountainous region of Glen Lyon in Perthshire. The very entrance to the glen is dramatic and awe-inspiring, beginning at Fortingall with the grey church standing guardian as it were against the forces of paganism that until very recently still had a considerable influence on the minds of the people. Two strange, water-worn stones, like great lions, guard the gate-posts of the sanctuary. In its precincts grows an ancient yew tree, believed to date back to the time of Pontius

Pilate who was allegedly born there while his father was on military service with the Roman army – a tall story no doubt, but suggestive of the antiquity of belief in this remote region. Going up the wild glen, the visitor cannot but note the fact that most of the houses have a pair of these strange stones – fashioned into fantastic shapes by their geological composition and the action of the fast-flowing waters of the River Lyon – set into their gateposts. They were believed to have both apotropaic powers and healing qualities. For the moment we shall pass by another important site of ancient cult practice until we come to the head of the valley where a large stretch of water now covers much of what was once the upper glen – this was carried out by the Hydro-Electricity Board. I had been told of a strange survival of Celtic paganism in the remote regions beyond the flooded territory by a colleague in the University of Edinburgh. It seemed to be so far-fetched, having all the elements of actual pagan practice that I determined to try to locate it.

The story was briefly as follows: a very long time ago, when the upper glen was still populated and centuries before the artificial loch had been made by flooding the floor of the valley below, there was an especially hard and severe winter. During the worst of the weather, a remarkable couple were observed coming towards the glen from the mountains. If the man was big, the woman was more than twice his size, and heavy with child. Now hospitality has always been regarded by the Celts of all periods as an essential moral duty. No strangers are turned away unfed and un-sheltered when food and shelter are required.

I have seen many examples of this unquestioning care for the traveller while living in the Outer Isles, in Skye, and in the mainland Highlands. It is a deeply-rooted, ancient code of behaviour; it is even mentioned in connection with the Celts by classical writers such as Diodorus Siculus, writing in the first century BC. His *Histories*, written between *c.*60–30 BC, in 40 books, contains accounts of Greece and Europe in Books 4-6. In Book 5 he gives this fascinating account of Celtic manners, one of several interesting observations: 'They also invite strangers to their banquets, and only after the meal do they ask who they are and of what they stand in need' (28,5). Things did not change easily in the Celtic world. Sadly, that is no longer the case, and the end of the past has very nearly been accomplished.

To return to the 'cult legend': the people of the upper glen, without hesitation, gave temporary shelter, food and drink to the huge couple while they began to build them a house which would be large enough to contain them. That night the woman gave birth to a girl-child. They were known as the *cailleach* ('hag' or 'goddess'), the *bodach* ('old man') and the *nighean* ('girl' or 'daughter'). They remained with their kind hosts for many years and repaid their trust and hospitality by bringing them good weather, plentiful crops, fat stock with a constant supply of rich milk, and game sufficient to satisfy the keenest of hunters. When they eventually left, as they had come, over the mountains, they were remembered in legend. This was still the case until the glen was flooded and the people left the upper region. But the shepherd remained, and it was his duty to see that the memory of this legendary couple was kept alive. A miniature stone house was at some time built *(21)*. Three river stones, worn into crude anthropomorphic form, were placed in the house *(plate 18)*.

On November Eve *(Samhain)*, the Celtic New Year, the thatch was removed from the Cailleach's house, and the large stones, which represented the three 'deities' were taken from their summer stance outside the house and placed within it. The entrance was closed up with stones, and every gap in the structure was filled with small stones, rushes and dry grasses so that it was draught-free and comfortable for the cold winter ahead. On the eve of 1 May *(Beltain)* more ritual observances were carried out. The two dates in question, 31 October (Eve of *Samhain*) and the eve of May Day (Eve of *Beltain*), mark the ancient divisions of the Celtic year and best befit a pastoral society. The Druids were extremely active at both festivals; each a fire celebration, and both being times of sacrifice and elaborate ritual which could bring about chaos and terror if they were not correctly observed and controlled by the Druids, mediators between the gods and mankind. In Upper Glen Lyon the shepherd had come to take the part of the Druid, being, in fact the guardian of the old cult and responsible for the correct perform-ance of ritual. To be ready to greet the first day of summer, the stones must be carefully washed in the rushy river. The stones and turves must be removed from the roof of the miniature house, to be replaced by a thatch of the rushes which grow plentifully, close by. The stones were then positioned facing down the glen towards Fortingall. Their presence was believed to ensure a good season for all things in the coming months. The shepherd, as guardian, had full responsibility for this remarkable ceremony. Both in summer and in winter, a large white quartz stone was placed on the roof of the miniature house. This could be seen gleaming bright from a good distance away and acted as an infallible 'marker' to travellers in search of the Cailleach's House.

Although I had been told of the existence of this miniature 'shrine' – but none of the 'cult' details – I found it difficult to believe, notwithstanding my personal knowledge of the Highlands and Islands and their traditions. With no forethought, but a strong determination to test the truth of the story, I set out with a colleague from Edinburgh one May Day. We decided to take the most direct route over the mountain from Bridge of Orchy, and found to our consternation that there was snow on the hill. Determined not to be discouraged, we kept going, and eventually saw the glen below us, where some snow still lay. Because of the quartz stone, perched like a great gull on the roof of the 'shrine' we were able to make straight for the site and there, indeed, were the stones, standing outside the house. The ritual had been faithfully observed. As we approached the structure in silence, we were both filled with a sense of trepidation. Kneeling down and looking inside the house, we observed two or three other smaller, but simi-larly-worked stones, fashioned by the action of the river into crude anthropomorphic shapes. There were also hazel nuts, which struck me as strange, as I could see no trees whatsoever in this part of the glen. We decided to take pictures of the site and of the stones. As the camera was pointed at the largest, the Cailleach herself, she began to fall forwards very slowly, and as she fell we could see that she had a face crudely worked and looking upwards to the skies. It was a creepy moment and indeed the whole atmosphere was strange. We also had to get back over the mountain-side before dark. It was difficult not to panic and we had the sensation of being watched, although the glen was totally devoid of habitation or any road. This feeling was, as it turned out, correct, because later, when I first met the shepherd – the first of many meetings – he told me that he had seen us coming and watched us closely until we had disappeared over the hill.

Perhaps the most interesting corroborative evidence for the antiquity of the cult of a local goddess is to be found in the place-names. The glen itself is called *Gleann na Cailliche*; the hill is *Beinn na Cailliche*; the stream is *Allt na Cailliche*, and the 'shrine' *Tigh na Cailliche*. In the wider area, a hill goddess was obviously venerated. She could be encountered driving her 'cattle' (deer) over the hills. Another shrine, dated to the Iron Age, was discovered some 20 miles away, near the ferry at Ballachulish. The wattled structure, fragmentary when found, housed the 5ft-high carved wooden image of a grim goddess, her eyes inlaid with pebbles of quartz. Her strap-like arms have five fingers of equal length and are positioned one above the other, over her stomach, perhaps indicating her powers of reproduction and fertility. This is now housed in the National Museum in Edinburgh. There are also river names in the form *Nigra Dea*, 'the Black Goddess' mentioned in Adamnán's Life of Columba, and a stream of this name flows into Loch Tay near Killin. The word 'black' used in such contexts, usually has the connotation of 'pagan'. The shepherd of Glen Lyon who became a close friend and told me many fascinating things about the old traditions of the district has recently passed away. The last contact I had with the glen described the Cailleach's House as being in a neglected state, indicating that with the passing of the shepherd the last guardian of the ancient cult had gone. A feeling of deep sadness

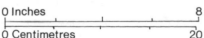

| 0 Inches | | 8 |

| 0 Centimetres | | 20 |

31 Celtic goddess,
possibly Epona, Alesia,
Côte-d'Or, France

can only be ameliorated by calling to mind the astonishing survival into the mid-twentieth century of the tradition which the shepherd had been so diligent in observing. I once asked him why he kept it going and he replied 'Because it has always been observed and it would be wrong not to do so.'

The second survival in the same glen in central Perthshire, Glen Lyon, must be considered next. It is very relevant to the subject-matter of this book and, in view of the general archaism of traditions in the whole of this region, should not be lightly dismissed. My informant, a local woman of high intelligence and integrity, proved to be a mine of information on many points of folklore and customs relating to the wider area of Tayside and Glen Lyon. One day she took me up to show me where, until before the First World

War and, vestigially, for some time afterwards, Beltain was cele-brated. She pointed out to me the place, some way up the glen, where annually a large square of ground was de-turfed. Here a great bonfire was lit, the material having been collected by the young men and boys of the community for some weeks previously. The people of the glen and those who could come from further afield used to gather in and around this square on May Day morning. It was an exciting time, a celebration of the beginning of summer which, like all seasons, was fraught with danger; bad weather would spoil the crops and affect the grazing; there was always the risk of disease; the yield of a good summer could quickly be blighted by an unfavourable harvest. The harvest, however, would be under the aegis of the great god Lugh (early 'Lugos', see illustration at head of Chapter 7) who inaugurated the festival known in Ireland as Lughnasa, another of the major quarterly festivals of the old Celtic year. Beltain, as the May festival was called in Ireland and Gaelic Scotland, was under the aegis of another pan-Celtic deity, Belenos (for which see Chapter 7 above). In Wales it was known as Calan Mai and earlier, as Calan Haf. In the Scottish Highlands Beltain marked the beginning of transhumance, when the cattle were moved to the high pastures where they would graze all summer. In Wales this was one of the *ysprydnos*, 'spirit nights'. All the calendar festivals were associated with the Druids, who in early times presided over the proceedings. In Ireland, they drove the cattle between two fires in order to purify them. This was perhaps the most important fire festival of the Celtic year.

To return to Glen Lyon, my informant told me that on May Day a huge fire was lit in the centre of the square. A special cake or scone was baked on a griddle. One portion of this was always found to be blackened. No one was seen to be responsible for this, but somehow the blackened portion always appeared. It was regarded as having been put there by some supernatural force or presence. When it was cooked, the bannock or scone was broken into small pieces. These were put into a bag and the person who got the blackened portion was regarded as the 'devoted' one, i.e. as the sacrificial victim, or scapegoat. He or she was made to jump three times over the glowing embers of the fire and then ritually driven out of the community. Portions of the bannock were thrown over the shoulder with such words, in Gaelic, as 'This I give to you, fox, spare my lambs' or 'This I give to you, ravens, spare my cattle'. There is a particularly interesting account of the festival of Beltain in Pennant's *Tour in Scotland*, Vol. 1, 1769. In view of its Druidic connotations, it is worth quoting the passage in full. Pennant is visiting Breadalbane, Perthshire. The first paragraph has a direct relevance to the question of lucky and unlucky days (for which see below).

Among the superstitious customs these are the most singular. A Highlander never begins any thing of consequence on the day of the week on which the third of May falls, which he styles *La Sheachanna na bleanagh*, or the dismal day, a day to be avoided. It is worth noting that in modern Gaelic, *la seachanta* means 'a disagreeable day'. On the first of May, the herdsmen of every village hold their Bel-tein, a rural sacrifice. (He adds this foot-note: 'My account of this, and every other ceremony mentioned in this journal, was communicated to me by gentlemen resident on the spot where they were performed'.) They cut a square trench on the ground, leaving the turf in the middle; on that they make a fire of wood, on which they dress a large caudle of eggs, butter, oatmeal and milk; and bring, besides the ingredients of the caudle, plenty of beer and whisky; for each of the company must contribute something. The rites begin with spilling some of the caudle on the ground by way of libation: on that, everyone takes a cake of oatmeal, upon which are raised nine square knobs, each dedicated to some particular being, the supposed preserver of their flocks and herds, or to some particu-lar animal, the real destroyer of them: each person then turns his face to the fire, breaks off a knob, and flinging it over his shoul-ders says. 'This I give to thee, preserve thou my horses; this to thee, preserve thou my sheep;' and so on. After that, they use the same ceremony to the noxious animals. 'This I give to you, oh

Fox! Spare thou my lambs; this to thee o hooded Crow! this to thee o Eagle!' When the ceremony is over, they dine on the caudle; and after the feast is finished, what is left is hid by two persons deputed for that purpose; but on the next Sunday they reassemble and finish the reliques of the first entertainment.

Glen Lyon is, of course, a part of Breadalbane. Written in 1769 by a fine and objective scholar the above account of Beltain in Breadalbane rings very true. Moreover, Pennant follows this account with some further information from another and distant part of the British Isles:

A custom, favouring of the Scotch Bel-tein, prevails in Gloucestershire, particularly about Newent and the neighbour-ing parishes, on the twelfth day, or on the Epiphany, in the evening. All the servants of every particular farmer assemble together in one of the fields that has been sown with wheat; on the border of which, in the most conspicuous or most elevated place, they make twelve fires of straw in a row; around one of which, made larger than the rest, they drink a cheerful glass of cyder to their master's health, success to the future harvest, and then returning home they feast on cakes made of caraways, etc. soaked in cyder, which they claim as a reward for their past labours in sowing the grain.

I have learnt of a very similar, but less elaborate Beltain celebration in Derbyshire, including the blackened bannock, and have been present there when the Beltain fires were blazing.

While we are in the company of Pennant we may note that he refers to:

an archaeological monument in Anglesey, a supreme consistory of Druidical administration, as the British names import (*Bryn-Gwyn at Tre'r Dryw*). Druidism having been the form of religion in this country before Christianity, the people still retain some superstitious customs of that Pagan religion. At Bel-tein on the first of May the herds of several farms gather dry wood, put fire to it, and dance three times southways about the pile. In the middle of June farmers go round their corn with burning torches, in memory of the 'Cerealis' [a festival in honour of Ceres, goddess of corn]. On Hallow Even they have several superstitious customs. At the full moon in March they cut withes of mistletoe or ivy, make circles of them, keep them all year, and pretend to cure hecticks and other troubles by them. And at marriages and baptisms they make a procession round the church, Deasoil, i.e. sunways, because the sun was the imme-diate object of the Druids' worship.

The most important account of the keeping of Beltain comes from Wales. It has much in common with the Glen Lyon ritual, but is even more detailed and convincing. The following version was recorded by Marie Trevelyan (1909, 22) who states that the last of the Beltain fires in the Vale of Glamorgan were kindled in the 1830s. The memory of the ancient custom lingered for much longer than that however, even when the finer details had become a memory. Her description is so detailed and so vivid that it is worth quoting it in full.

The fire was done in this way: nine men would turn their pockets inside out and see that every piece of money and all metals were off their persons. Then the men went into the nearest woods, and collected sticks of nine different kinds of trees. These were carried to the spot where the fire had to be built. There a circle was cut in the sod, and the sticks were set crosswise. All around the circle the people stood and watched the proceedings. One of the men would then take two bits of oak, and rub them together until a flame was kindled. This was applied to the sticks, and soon a large fire was made. Sometimes two fires were set up side by side. These fires, whether one or two, were called *coelcerth* or bonfires. Round cakes of oatmeal and brown meal were split in four and placed in a small flour-bag, and everybody present had to pick out a portion. The last bit in the bag fell to the lot of the bag-holder. Each person who chanced to pick up a piece of the brown-meal cake was compelled to leap three times over the flames, or to run thrice between the two fires, by which means the people thought they were sure of a plentiful harvest. Shouts and screams of those who had to face the ordeal could be heard ever so far, and those who chanced to pick the oatmeal portions sang and danced and clapped their hands in approval, as the holders of the brown bits leaped three times over the flames, or ran three times between the two fires. As a rule, no danger attended these curious celebrations, but occasionally somebody's clothes caught fire, which was quickly put out ... I have also heard my grandfather say that in times gone by the people would throw a calf in the fire when there was any disease among the herds. The same would be done with a sheep if there was anything the matter with a flock. I can remember myself seeing cattle being driven between the two fires to 'stop the disease spreading'. When in later times it was not considered humane to drive the cattle between the fires, the herdsmen were accustomed to force the animals over the wood ashes to protect them against various ailments ... People carried the ashes left after these fires to their homes, and a charred brand was not only effectual against pestilence, but magical in its use. A few of the ashes placed in a person's shoes protected the wearer from any great sorrow or woe.

(Owen, 1987, 97-8)

There are many other Beltain customs which go directly back to the time of the Druids when they drove the cattle through two great fires, sacred to the pan-Celtic god, Belenos. Hallowe'en, the Eve of 1 November and one of the three Welsh *ysprydnosau* (spirit nights), was a time of darkness and chaos, when the gods played tricks on mankind and danger lurked in every corner of the landscape. Illusion was employed by the tricky gods to mislead and terrify. It still remains a frightening night in many places, and in my own family it was always kept. It too was a fire festival. The great *Feis* or Feast of Tara, seat of the kings of Ireland, was held on this ominous date. The dead were believed to rise from their graves and their spirits to walk the earth; the *sídh* mounds were opened up so that bold or unwary people could enter them.

The Coligny Calendar

The veneration of the moon can be traced to the early Celtic world, where the people measured time by means of the moon, and called themselves 'sons of the god of night'. They counted their days by the preceding night, and were very conscious of the different stages of the moon which are so magically revealed.

> The Gauls all assert their descent from Dis pater and say that it is the Druidic belief. For this reason they count periods of time not by the number of days but by the number of nights; and in reckoning birthdays and the new moon and new year their unit of reckoning is the night followed by the day.
>
> (Caesar, *De Bello Gallico*)

The complex and fascinating Druidic calendar, discovered in a fragmentary state in 1897 in silvan country at Coligny, which lies some 15 miles to the north-east of Bourg-en-Bresse, Ain, France, is an early example of Celtic calendrical skill and facility for mathematics and the sciences which the classics did not fail to record. Like other ancient priesthoods, the Druids, in one of their complex personae, may rightly be termed astronomer-priests. The find spot is interesting, for one must presume that this was always a silvan region and the Druids chose to worship in groves of trees; other sites were not, of course, excluded. The Coligny calendar is highly complex and is dated to the first or second centuries AD, to a time when Roman persecution of the order was at its height.

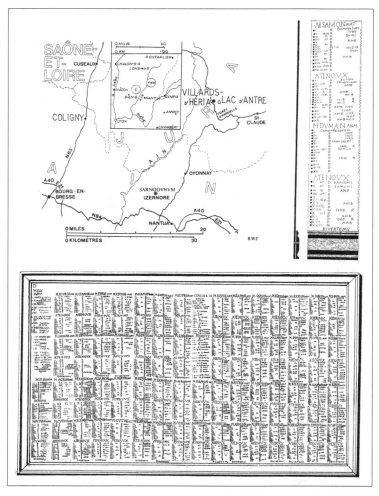

32 Calendars, Coligny, Ain, and Villards-d'Héria, Jura – site map; extract from Coligny calendar; impression of original appearance of Cligny calendar

We consider this situation in greater detail when considering the classical evidence for the Druids and Druidism. The Coligny calendar is certainly an impressive document, even in its damaged state. The fragments of the great bronze panel, which is engraved with a fascinating calendrical table, are housed in Lyon. There is a fine copy of it in the National Library of Wales, in Aberystwyth. The calendar consisted of an engraved bronze plate measuring some 5ft in width and about 3ft 5ins in height with a moulded frame. It is an invaluable antiquity and confirms various aspects of Druidic practice and custom in the ancient Celtic world which are attested from other sources. Its complexity testifies to the mathematical and astronomical skills of this learned order. It is a remarkable document, dating to a time when inscriptions in a Celtic language have not often survived, and it is remarkably informative. That it is not unique is attested by the discovery of an even more fragmentary calendar from approximately the same area of France, about 20 miles from Coligny, a place called Villards-d'Héria, Jura (Duval et Pinault). If these calendars were displayed in temples, as one might suppose, we must perhaps envisage some refinement of structure, and possibly other astronomical and calendrical features. The calendar displays 16 columns of months and covers a period of 5 years. These lists were divided from each other by lines designated by small holes running vertically from top to bottom. It had been broken, deliberately, or because the holes had weakened the metal, into about two hundred pieces of which about half were recovered at the end of the nineteenth century.

The illustration (32) suggests the appearance of the calendar when it was intact. Each month is divided into two columns or blocks by the word ATENOUX. The Gaelic word for night is *nochd*, the Welsh *nos*. Atenoux may mean something like 'returning night'. There are fifteen days in the first group and fourteen or fifteen days in the second. The lettering and the numerals are Roman but the language is unequivocally Celtic. The second part of *Fig. 32* shows two of the sixty months covered by the Coligny calendar. These are the only two which can be assembled in their complete form from seven pieces which formed part of the fourth column of the calendar. The months are SAMON, a thirty day month followed by the word *mat* ('good'), Gaelic *math*; and DUMAN, a month of twenty-nine days followed by the word *anm* ('not good'). This distinction would seem to apply to the days of the month as well, and a knowledge of lucky or unlucky days was professed by the Druids of Ireland and such a belief survived in Gaelic Scotland, as no doubt elsewhere in the Celtic world, namely, that some days were unlucky or bad while others were good.

There are many charms and incantations in Alexander Carmichael's great collection of lore of the Highlands and Islands, dealing with lucky and unlucky days. An example of this superstition occurs in a sad charm published in Yorkshire Celtic Studies by his grandson, James Carmichael Watson. It is entitled *Latha Sealbhach*, 'The Prosperous or Lucky Day'. A young boy is preparing to leave the island of Benbecula and seek his fortune in the 'wrangling' *(carraideach)* world outside. It was a terrible time for mothers especially as there was no future for young people in their native Highlands and Islands except for the eldest who would inherit such home and land as his parents possessed. The parents knew that they were unlikely to see their boys again for many years, if ever. Before setting out on his long journey the youth would have to consult his mother as to which would be the best day for his departure. 'What day now, mother, shall I go? What is the auspicious day of the week at all'? Then the mother of the youth answered and spoke the words that follow:

> Thou man who wouldst travel tomorrow,
> tarry a little as thou art,
> till I make a shirt of thread for thee;
> there is waiting and waiting for that;
> the lint was sown but has not grown,
> the wool is on the sheep of the wasteland,
> the loom is in the wood of Patrick,
> the beam is in the highest tree,
> the shuttle is with the King of Spain,

> The bobbin is with the Queen,
> the weaver is not born to her mother.
> Thou man who wouldst travel tomorrow,
> thou shalt not go on Monday
>   nor shalt thou go on Tuesday.
> Wednesday is tormenting, hurtful,
> On Thursday are temptation and turbulence
> Friday is a day of rest,
> Saturday is to the Mary Mother,
> Let the Lord's Day praise the High king,
> Thou man who wouldst travel strongly,
> thou shalt not go on Monday (Wednesday),
>   the end of the quarter.
> Thou man who wouldst travel,
> there is red blood upon thy shirt;
> not blood of roe nor blood of deer,
> but blood of thy body and thou full of wounds.

Having made this gloomy prognostication in which no day at all was auspicious for her young son to travel and leave her probably forever, the poor woman ensured that he would *never* leave her and would 'close her eyes when she went over the black river of death'.

This passage can be to some extent paralleled in an early Irish heroic tale, the remarkable and lengthy account of the *Táin Bó Cúailnge*, 'The Cattle Raid of Cooley'. The story has for hero the remarkable Ulster youth, Cú Chulainn, whose divine father is the god Lugh. The characters are divine or semi-divine, the events dramatic and bloody. The tale is concerned with a great battle between the men of Connacht and the men of Ulster over a divine bull *(plate 15)*, in origin a swineherd transformed by magic together with his fellow herd into a series of existences in different shapes, but always retaining their human understanding and reason. This is very much a Druidic belief, that of metempsychosis, and the entire tale is concerned with gods and Druids, prophecy and magic. The bulls were called the Brown of Cuailnge and the Finnbennach of Connacht. The Finnbennach was owned by Ailill, King of Connacht, and his wife Medb coveted this exceptionally fine animal. She seeks out a bull of equal quality and is told that there is such a bull in Ulster, namely the Donn of Cuailnge. She determines to gain possession of this bull; a great battle between Connacht and Ulster ensues, and after much slaughter Ulster is victorious and the brown bull savages his rival and scatters his bodily parts widely over the countryside.

Many of the early Irish scholars had become Christianised, but still had a deep respect and affection for the old traditions of their land. There is a rather moving postscript to the great epic tale (O'Rahilly, 1967):

> A blessing on everyone who shall faithfully memorise the Táin as it is written here and shall not add any other form to it.
>
> But I who have written this story, or rather this fable, give no credence to the various incidents related in it. For some things in it are the deceptions of demons, others poetic figments; some are probable, others improbable; while still others are intended for the delectation of foolish men.

The story is known to have existed in the eighth century and its origin could probably have been earlier. It depicts a heroic society, some aspects of which may belong, in origin, to the Celtic Iron Age. The oral memory, deliberately and assiduously cultivated in the early Celtic world, conditioned society to use their memories rather than to rely upon the written word, and much of our earliest Celtic literature must have been correct, in some form or another and to some degree, long after social conditions had changed and the world had become more readily accessible to scholars, travellers and traders alike. The great queen of Connacht, Medb, whose name means 'intoxication' (hence 'mead', the heady drink which is so popular in these early tales), wanted to make war on Ulster because her request for one of the divine bulls, Donn Cúailnge, 'Lord' (or

'Brown One') of Cúailnge had been refused. She gathered her troops and they spent the next two weeks at Rath Cruachan (13), the royal seat, feasting and drinking and refreshing themselves before the battle. Medb sought out her Druid and asked him to foresee and prophesy the outcome of the approaching conflict. She asked to know who will return from the foray. He replied 'Whoever comes or comes not back, you yourself will come.' The driver turned the chariot and Medb returned. She saw in front of her a 'wonder'. A woman was approaching her, weaving a fringe on a rich and elaborate loom. She wore a fine cloak fastened by a round, heavy-headed brooch. She was Fedelm, the prophetess who had been away in Britain, learning the arts of prophecy and Druidism. She told Medb she is the prophetess from Sid Cruachna. Fedelm prophesied nothing but blood and disaster if Medb embarked with her troops on the cattle-raid. Medb asked her 'But speak the truth to us Fedelm. Oh Fedelm Prophetess, how do you see our army?' 'I see red on them, I see crimson.' Then she uttered her prophecy and foretold the coming of the great Ulster hero, Cú Chulainn, 'Hound of Culann'. Culann was a smith; the profession held high status in Celtic society because of his power over the 'magic' metal, iron, the substance that kept at bay the fairies and evil spirits. 'Blood will flow from heroes' bodies. Long will it be remembered.' This dramatic and evocative early Irish epic seems a far cry from the grieving mother trying to prevent the departure of her beloved son. But she too prophesied blood. The youth, like Medb, seeks to learn the auspicious day for his departure from his homeland, but his mother tells him that all days are inauspicious and foresees blood, as does Fedelm – 'not blood of roe nor blood of deer, but blood of thy body and thou full of wounds'. Unlike the son, Medb, headstrong and passionate as always, chooses to ignore the dire warning of the prophetess and plunges headlong into a ghastly defeat.

One of the most impressive examples of the auspicious or inauspicious day occurs at a later stage of the Táin which has already been mentioned in connection with the prophetess Fedelm. It takes us back to the days before Cú Chulainn was an heroic warrior, when he was a precocious lad, having the growth and powers of a boy of fourteen while he was barely seven. He had been christened *Sétanta mac Súaltaim*. (Súaltaim was his 'earthly' father; Lugh the god was his divine father); Cú Chulainn was a nephew of the king, Conchobor mac Nessa, his mother being Dechtire, Conchobor's sister. The royal stronghold was at Navan Fort (Emain Macha), where important archaeological excavations have taken place in recent years.

Shortly after Cú Chulainn had earned his new name an event was to take place which set the seal on his career as a great warrior. Hardly eight years of age, the boy was playing with his hurley stick and ball close to where the Druid Cathbad was teaching his pupils to the north-east of Emain and he had eight pupils from his class of Druidic learning with him. One of these asked his master what omen there was for that day; was it auspicious or inauspicious? The Druid replied that the boy who should take up arms on that day would be famous, but his life would be short. Cú Chulainn heard this augury. He threw his childish playthings away and went to the king's private chamber. 'What do you want little one? asked the king. 'To take arms' replied the lad. 'Who told you to do that boy?' asked the king. 'Cathbad the Druid' replied the little lad. 'He would not deceive you,' said the king, and gave him a set of weapons. So, because of the omens read by the Druid, Cú Chulainn's fate was sealed, and Ulster acquired an invincible warrior and protector.

There are many other examples throughout the Celtic tradition of the reading of omens, and the Coligny calendar demonstrates just how fundamental and vital to the Celts were the auspicious and inauspicious days, a superstition that has survived down to our own time. Until the First World War (1914-18), there was an extremely rich corpus of folklore material readily available to the collector. Fenian traditions, that is, stories connected with the ultimately divine Fionn Mac Cumhaill – known as the Fionn Cycle of Story Telling – were still commonplace up to the time of the First World War and fragments of these persist down to our own time. Stories about the Tuatha Dé Danann have always been less prolific in the folk traditions of Ireland and Scotland, but I was privileged to hear a fragment of the Táin delivered orally by an old crofter in the Island of Skye while collecting surviving traces of ancient custom and belief. Many of these archaic stories are chanted and, as the excitement builds up, so does the voice rise and the speed quicken. I shall always remember this particular informant, his voice rising almost to a screech as he cried: *'mharbh iad an Donn Árd, mharbh iad an Donn Árd!'* ('They have killed the noble brown one, they have killed the noble brown one!'). The bull here is clearly the Brown Bull of Cuailnge who slew his rival, the White-Horned Finnbennach, related above. Both bulls were originally divine swineherds, who underwent many metamorphoses.

With the loss of so many young men from rural Celtic areas (and areas which although conquered by the Romans in the early centuries of our era had still retained numerous folk memories of our distant, native past) folk customs were inevitably made redundant. In terms of annual calendar events, some clearly of considerable antiquity, became seriously affected and many died out, some to be deliberately revived later in the century. However, the importance of survival as opposed to revival, must have been the complete spontaneity with which certain ancient festivals were reenacted and the enthusiasm of entire communities of people who participated in these events. A good deal of folklore of an archaic kind survived in spite of the loss of those who had been taught by their parents and grandparents to enact the old legends and to recite often lengthy and complex tales and poems of a heroic nature. The coming of the Second World War in 1939 dealt a much more serious blow to the oral survival of the past. The ensuing decades – especially from the middle of the twentieth century on, with distractions such as television and computer technology – saw a rapid decline in both the spoken Celtic languages and the repertoire of folklore and ancient custom that still existed, and, in part, had depended upon them.

When I was doing fieldwork on this theme in Co. Cavan, in central northern Ireland, my friend and colleague, the late T.J.

Barron, former headmaster of Bailieboro School, Co. Cavan, gave me an interesting little booklet published in 1937 by the Irish Folklore Commission, under the aegis of the Department of Education for the information of Managers and Teachers of National Schools. The date is worth noting. It begins with the following instruction:

> The collection of the oral traditions of the Irish people is a work of national importance. It is but fitting that in our primary schools the senior pupils should be invited to participate in the task of rescuing from oblivion the traditions which, in spite of the vicissitudes of the historic Irish nation, have, century in and century out, been preserved with loving care by their ancestors. The task is an urgent one for in our time most of this important national oral heritage will have passed away for ever.

The booklet goes on to state:

> In the same way, customs and beliefs, which in a conservative country like ours come down from the Bronze Age, as well as from our Early Christian Period, will throw light on our relations with the outside world during these two periods of our history ... In writing down these traditions the standpoint should be taken that this is the first time, and perhaps the last, that they will be recorded.

Then follows a comprehensive list of subjects and items to be collected in the field, including hero tales and, most importantly, tales of the legendary Fianna, or Fenians as they are called in English. Alexander Carmichael's Carmina Gadelica, a work of great value and devotion, was collected from the people of the Western Highlands and Islands of Scotland, in the Scottish Gaelic language. Volumes 1 and 2 were published in 1900 and 1928. Volumes 3 and 4 were edited by James Carmichael Watson, the collector's grandson, and were published in 1940 and 1941. A further volume was published posthumously – 'James Carmichael Watson ... regarded the completion of Carmina Gadelica as of the greatest importance, and before enlisting in the Royal Navy in 1941 he made provision for ensuring that the work would be continued should he himself be prevented from returning to it.' Tragically he was killed in action while serving in the Royal Navy, in 1942. The late Professor Angus Matheson undertook the enormous task of preparing Volume 5 for publication in 1954. Professor Matheson states that the volume would contain 'a large body of prose and verse concerning fairies and other supernatural beings; some miscellaneous poetry; proverbs, riddles, and similar lore'. There is an interesting comment that the poetry was intended to be sung (or chanted). It was used in the past to avert serious crises, such as might occur at any time in this touchy, quick and boastful society, where any hint of an insult would result in an instantaneous armed response. A good example of such behaviour occurs in the story of the Drunkenness of the Ulstermen, set out in full in Chapter 7 above.

EPILOGUE

The Celts were, at the height of their powers, the masters of Europe. Where their origins lie is still in question – as Henri Hubert, that fine scholar, says, 'Was it in the west, in Ireland, or in Central Europe, in the Danube region?' As another great scholar, the late Professor Stuart Piggott, used to say, 'If you could have taken an aeroplane in the Iron Age and flown from the Baltic to the Mediterranean, and from the Black Sea to the west of Ireland, your whole journey would have been over Celtic-occupied terrain.'

The Celts clearly evolved their culture from peoples whose history is far beyond the reach of the historian. We may now make some progress in this field using the dramatic results of an ever-developing archaeological expertise, aided by modern technology of various kinds. The Celts spread, within the period of the early historical records, far east into Galatia (2). Their mercenary soldiers, who were such a feature of Celtic society; those tall, blond, vain, naked and fearless fighting men the Gaesatae, 'Spear-bearers', caused terror throughout the western world. Whole tribes, with their inevitable complement of Druids, Bards and Fili, members of the ancient tripartite learned Order, conquered and settled far and wide. Only one tribe, in Iberia, left the record of its own name: *Celtici*, which appears on the earliest classical maps (25). Apart from the predictable Celtic names of many natural features in this area, such as those of rivers, hills, etc., we have evidence for the earliest use of three important Celtic words which are still, in their various forms, common today in Celtic languages, namely: *dunum* ('fort'); *magus* ('plain'; Irish *magh,* Welsh *maes*); *briga* ('height' or 'hill'; Irish *brí,* Welsh *bre, brig*).

Druids seem not to be mentioned by name in Iberia, but as Salisbury says in her brilliant study (1985), there were Iberian 'holy men' and it seems, as these tribes were Celts, they would hardly be lacking a priesthood, and from the description we have of British Druids, they seemed to combine both ritual and pastoral functions. Their knowledge of important rituals would have been derived from years of study, yet they seemed to have supernatural powers, which would strongly suggest that they were in fact the Celt-Iberian Druids.

The Celt-Iberians worshipped the moon, as did the Celts in general, and held many of their beliefs in common. Later, classical history adds veracity to speculation. Most important are the considerable numbers of stone heads which closely resemble many of those found widely in the other Celtic countries. Moreover, there are splendid stone carvings of boars *(32)* and bulls from central Spain and northern Portugal, generally associated with the hillforts of Celtic or partly Celtic tribes, and it has been suggested that these have to do with the prosperity and safe-keeping of the herds. They are rather larger than life and from northern Portugal there are sculptures of warriors bearing round shields, and wearing short, thigh-length tunics, also of tall warriors about 5ft 10ins in height and these, too would be protective figures, keeping at bay any enemies.

In the West, whole tribes moved into Asia Minor to become masters of huge tracts of land *(2).* Their chief sanctuary, *Drunemeton* ('Oak/Druid Sanctuary') provides testimony for the Gaulish religion surviving, as does the fact that, when the three Galatian tribes met at the great annual assembly at this sanctuary, their dogs were garlanded with flowers and there was much festive activity. The season can be guessed at, but the choice can be only twofold:

33 Boar hunt on four-wheeled platform, Merida, Badajoz, Spain, second – first centuries BC

Beltain (1 May), when flowers are at their pristine best, would seem to be a first choice; the other festival is Lughnasa (1 August) but this perhaps seems less likely. The May festival was originally in honour of the god Belenos, who was worshipped over wide areas of Britain and Europe. In the first – second century AD we know that high-ranking Celts officiated, probably as priests, in the great temple at Pessinos. As we do not know where this *nemeton* was situated, and as it was of major importance both for ritual and administrative purposes, it is not improbable that it was near, or incorporated in, the great Temple of Pessinos, where the Celtic nobles held high priestly office and/or contributed to the temple upkeep, this indicating that they participated in Galatian, as well as their own religious cults. The Galatians are referred to with some asperity by St Paul in his famous *Letter to the Galatians*, remarking

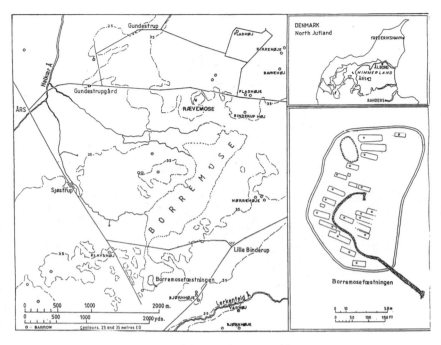

34 Site of the Gundestrup cauldron

that they had so soon given up their faith to return to their ancient festivals: 'O foolish Galatians, who has bewitched you? *(Galatians, III, 1)*... Now, after ye have known God, or rather, are known of God, how turn ye again to the weak and beggarly elements whereunto ye desire again to be in bondage? *Ye observe days, and months, and times, and years* [my emphasis]. ...' *(Galatians, IV, 10-11)*. St Paul was writing in the first century AD *(33)*; some three centuries later St Jerome, travelling in Galatia, commented that the people spoke a language (Gaulish) as pure as that spoken by the Treveri of Gaul.

Unlike the Irish Druids, the Druids of Gaul would seem not to have fought in battle although it was not apparently forbidden to them to do so. They did, however, take part in exhorting the naked

warriors and spurring them on to victory. Their lack of clothing in
battles was mistakenly interpreted by their enemies as arrogant
boastfulness. In fact, they believed that the state of nakedness was
pleasing to the gods – the *sacredness* of nakedness. In Ireland, the
Druids seemed to be fully involved in the warfare to which the
tribes were so powerfully addicted. They certainly rushed about,
shouting imprecations at the enemy and exhorting their own tribe
to victory. They used potent spells and adopted magical postures,
such as the *corrguinecht* referred to in Chapter 1, and many other
forms of destructive magic. Although the Druids were believed
not to take part in actual fighting, it would certainly seem that,
during their long period of training, the use of weapons and the
ability to fend for themselves in the wilderness, must have been
taught. There was in Gaul, as in Ireland, one Druid above all others,
known as the Archdruid. We learn from the classics (Caesar, VI, 13)
that, in the event of this position becoming vacant and if there was
no clear-cut successor to this high office, the two most likely
candidates would even resort to weapons and single combat in
order to decide the case.

To return to Ireland, we have one very clear example of a Druid
who was also a practising warrior. Cathbad, the great Ulster Druid,
one night left Ulster with three times nine men and went on a raid
through Erin. He was a man of knowledge and Druidical skill; he
was also endowed with great bodily strength. There was a young
girl called Assa (meaning 'docile' or 'gentle'), and this story, which
is entitled *The Birth of Conchobor*, tells how she was the daughter of
the king of Ulster and, like her male contemporaries, she was
required by her father to undergo a full programme of education.
In accordance with his wishes, she had been trained by 12 tutors
and she was a docile and receptive pupil. One night Cathbad,
during his foray through Erin, slew, with his own hand, these
tutors. The tutors were also the girl's guardians. She was shocked
and outraged by this brutal killing, but she had no idea who had
perpetrated the terrible deed. She took to arms herself and, with
her companions, set out to discover the perpetrator. From that

moment, her name changed from Assa ('gentle') to Nessa ('ungentle'). She destroyed and plundered and became a brilliant warrior. Once she had gone into the countryside and her companions were preparing food; she saw a spring of water, and she went to bathe in it. While she was bathing, Cathbad passed by and saw her, and he bared his sword above her head, and stood between her and her clothing and weapons. She called for mercy and he said he would grant it only on condition that she should be true to him for as long as he lived and that she would be his one and only wife. They went to her father, who made them welcome and gave them land, and she bore him a son, Conchobor. Thus, although the Druids were not *warriors*, there is nothing to suggest that they were banned from the use of arms.

Christianity, and the battle between Christian zeal and Druidic magic, was seen not to conflict to any great extent with the pagan ideal – 'Worship the gods (God), tell the truth, be manly.' Druids were a problem: in their pagan form, they could not be countenanced. Thus some Druids undoubtedly converted to Christianity and even entered the church; others gave up the practice of magic and merged with the File who did not excite Christian opprobrium. They were able – in conjunction with the Bards (with their awesome powers of satire and their coveted ability to bestow or make fame (Welsh *clod,* Gaelic *cliú)* for their patrons) – to survive, and so the old orders continued in modified form, under a new guise. Ancient feuds, however, continued; new learning and influences from other lands penetrated Ireland. But fighting was second nature to these people, whose many talents were marred by the instability of their deeply-ingrained prejudices. The Druids virtually created the 'Celtic mind' and we can still detect this in the continuing passion for poetry, fluent language, riddles and veneration of both God and of the poet. The so-called 'Druidic Revival' based on Stonehenge, has been expertly and elegantly discussed by the late Professor Stuart Piggott. That great enigmatic monument standing dramatically on the Wiltshire plain, is still popularly regarded as the focal point of ancient Druidism.

Whether or not the developing science of archaeology and new discoveries will provide the necessary evidence to justify this association remains to be seen; however, it is in the Welsh *Eisteddfodau* that convincing glimpses of the true influence of Druidism can yet be discerned. The word originally connoted 'an assembly of poets'. The early *eisteddfod* consisted of a gathering of poets belonging to the Bardic Order, and its aim was to control the conduct of the profession, to establish the rules of metre and to grant licences to those poets who had completed the requisite stages of their apprenticeship. This was in order to regularise the profession. The most important of these *eisteddfodau* were held at Carmarthen in 1451, and at Caerwys in 1523 and 1567. After this, the tradition degenerated. The *eisteddfod* was revived on a provincial basis during the nineteenth century and it was during the 1860s that the National Eisteddfod Society was formed. The event now attracts huge crowds of both participants and spectators. The competitions include singing and recitation; the most highly esteemed event is the recitation of poetry and the award by the Archdruid of the Bardic Crown for the most outstanding poem. Here in this latter-day event in Wales, we can discern the traces of cultural and spiritual proclivities, first encountered in the perceptive comments of the classical writers and elaborated in the later records of Ireland and Wales, to which we are indebted for such a rich portrayal of these elements – which, unpredictably, and in spite of many adverse factors, did so much to create the enduring Celtic mind.

BIBLIOGRAPHY

Barber, J., *et al.*, 1989, An Unusual Iron Age Burial at Hornish Point, South Uist, in *Antiquity,* 63, 773.

Bromwich, R., 1992, *Trioedd Ynys Prydein, The Welsh Triads*, University of Wales Press.

Brunaux, J-L., 1998, *The Celtic Gauls,* London.

Chapman, A., 1998, Brack Mills, Northampton, an early Iron Age torc, in *Current Archaeology,* 159, 92ff.

Chivite, J. T., 1965, *Escultura Celto-Romana,* Vigo.

Cross, T. P. and Slover, C. H., 1936, *Ancient Irish Tales*, London.

Cunliffe, B., 1997, *The Ancient Celts,* O.U.P.

Duval, P. M., Pinault, G., 1988, Les Calendriers Coligny et Villards-d'Héria, in *Recueil des Inscriptions Gauloises*, Paris, XIII., pp. 442ff

Gray, E. (ed.), 1982, *The Second Battle of Mag Tuired* (Moytura), Irish Texts Society, Dublin.

Grooms, C., 1993, *Cewri Cymru, The Giants of Wales*, The Edward Mellen Press, Lewiston, Queenstown, Lampeter.

Jones, G., Jones, T., 1949, *The Mabinigion,* London.

Kelly, F., 1988, *A Guide to Early Irish Law*, Dublin.

Kendrick, T. D., 1927, *The Druids*, London.

Koch, J. T., Carey, J., 1995, *The Celtic Heroic Age*, Massachussetts.

Lambrechts, P., 1954, *L'Exaltation de la Tête dans la Pensée et dans l'Art des Celtes*, Bruges.

Leeds, E. T., 1930, A Bronze Cauldron from the River Cherwell, Oxfordshire, in *Archaeologia*, LXXX, 1-36.

Le Roux, F., Guyonvarc'h, C.-J., 1986, *Les Druides*, Rennes.

McGrath, F., 1979, *Education in Ancient and Medieval Ireland*, Dublin.

McManus, D., 1991, *Guide to Ogam*, Maynooth.

MacNeill, M., 1962, *The Festival of Lughnasa*, O.U.P.

Martin, M., 1716, 1970, *A Description of the Western Isles of Scotland*, Edinburgh.

Mitchell, S., 1993, *Anatolia*, vol. 1 O.U.P.

Nagy, J.F., 1955, *Wisdom of the Outlaw*

O'Curry, E., 1878, *Lectures on the MS Material of Ancient Irish History*, Dublin.

O'Rahilly, C., ed., 1967, *Táin Bó Cúailnge from the Book Of Leinster*, Dublin.

Owen, T.M., 1987, *Welsh Folk Customs*, Llandysul.

Piggott, S., 1968, *The Druids*, London.

Powel, T.G.E., 1958 and 1980, *The Celts*, London.

Price, G. ed, 1998, *Encyclopedia of the Languages of Europe*, Oxford.

Raftery, B., 1994, *Pagan Celtic Ireland*, London.

Reeves, W., ed., 1988 *Adamnán, Life of Columba*, Llanerch.

Ross, A., Feachem, R.W., 1976, Pits, Shafts and Wells, Sanctuaries of the Belgic Britons?, in *Studies in Ancient Europe*, Leicester.

Ross, A., Feachem, R.W., 1984, Heads Baleful and Benign, in Miket, R., Burgess, C., ed., *Between and Beyond the Walls*, Edinburgh.

Ross, A., 1986, *Lindow Man and the Celtic Tradition*, in Stead, I., *et al.*, *The Body in The Bog*, London.

Ross, A., 1988, Severed Heads and sacred waters, in *Source*, NS no 5, 4-11.

Ross, A. 1967, 1992, *Pagan Celtic Britain*, London.

Sherley-Price, L., 1970, *Bede, A History of the English Church and People*, Harmondsworth.

Suppe, F., 1989, The Cultural Significance of Decapitation in High Medieval Wales and the Marches, in *Bulletin of the Board of Celtic Studies*. Vol 36, 147-160.

Srejovic, D., 1972, *Lepenski Vir*, New York and London.

Stead, I., 1998, *The Salisbury Hoard*, Tempus.

Thorpe, G., 1978, *Giraldus Cambrensis, The Journey into Wales*, London

Tierney, J.J., 1960, The Celtic Ethnography of Posidonius, in *Proceedings of the Royal Irish Academy LX(C)*, 189-275.

Trevelyan, M., 1909, *Folklore and Customs of Wales*, Cardiff.

White, H.G.E., 1968, *Ausonius vol. 1*, Loeb Classics.

Williams, I., Bromwich, R., 1972, *Armes Prydein, The Prophecy of Britain*, Dublin.

FURTHER READING

Chapman, A., 1998. Brack Mill, Northampton, an early Iron Iron Age torc, in *Current Archaeology*, 159, 92ff.

Duval, P-M. and Pinault, G., 1988, Les Calendriers Coligny et Villards-d'Héria, in *Recueil des Inscriptions Gauloises*, Paris, XIII, pp 442ff.

Gray, E. (ed.), 1982, *The Second Battle of Mag Tuired (Moytura)*, Irish Texts Society, LII.

Green, M.J., 2002, *Dying for the Gods: Human Sacrifice in Iron Age and Roman Europe*, Tempus.

Jones, G. and Jones, T., 1991, *The Mabinogion*, London and Vermont.

MacNeill, M., 1962, *The Festival of Lughnasa,* OUP.

Piggott, S., 1968, *The Druids*, London.

Powell, T.G.E., *The Celts*, 1958 & 1980, London.

Raftery, B., 1994, *Pagan Celtic Ireland*, London.

Ross, A., 1992, *Pagan Celtic Britain*, London.

Salisbury, J., 1985, *Iberian Popular Religion 600BC to AD700*, Vol 20, The Edwin Mellen Press, Lewiston, Queenstown, Lampeter.

Sherley-Price, L., 1970, *Bede, A History of the English Church and People*, Harmondsworth.

Tierney, J.J., 1960, The Celtic Ethnography of Posidonius, *Proceedings of the Royal Irish Academy* LX(C), 189-275.

INDEX

TEMPUS – REVEALING HISTORY

D-Day
The First 72 Hours
WILLIAM F. BUCKINGHAM
'A compelling narrative'
The Observer
£9.99
0 7524 2842 X

London
A HISTORICAL COMPANION
'A readable and reliable work of reference that
deserves a place on every Londoner's bookshelf'
Stephen Inwood
£20
0 7524 3434 9

The London Monster
Terror on the streets in 1790
JAN BONDESON
'Gripping'
The Guardian
£9.99
0 7524 3327 X

M: MI5's First Spymaster
ANDREW COOK
'Well-researched, penetrating and engaagingly
written'
Andrew Roberts
£20
0 7524 2896 9

Agincourt A New History
ANNE CURRY
'A highly distinguished and convicing account of
one of the decisive battles of the Western world'
Christopher Hibbert
£25
0 7524 2828 4

The English Resistance
The Underground war Against the Normans
PETER REX
'An invaluable rehabilitation of an ignored resist-
ance movement'
The Sunday Times
£17.99
0 7524 2827 6

William II Rufus, The Red King
EMMA MASON
'A thoroughly new appraisal of a much maligned
king. The dramatic story of his life is told with
great pace and insight'
John Gillingham
£25
0 7524 3528 0

Elizabeth Wydeville The Slandered Queen
ARLENE OKERLUND
'A penetrating, thorough and wholly convincing
vindication of this unlucky queen'
Sarah Gristwood
£18.99
0 7524 3384 9

TEMPUS – REVEALING HISTORY

Quacks
Fakers and Charlatans in Medicine
ROY PORTER
'A delightful book'
The Daily Telegraph
£12.99
0 7524 2590 0

The Tudors
RICHARD REX
'Up-to-date, readable and reliable. The best introduction to England's most important dynasty'
David Starkey
£9.99
0 7524 3333 4

The Kings & Queens of England
MARK ORMROD
'Of the numerous books on the kings and queens of England, this is the best'
Alison Weir
£9.99
0 7524 2598 6

The Covent Garden Ladies
Pimp General Jack & the Extraordinary Story of Harris's List
HALLIE RUBENHOLD
'Has all the atmosphere and edge of a good novel… magnificent'
Frances Wilson
£20
0 7524 2850 0

Okinawa 1945
GEORGE FEIFER
'A great book… Feifer's account of the three sides and their experiences far surpasses most books about war'
Stephen Ambrose
£17.99
0 7524 3324 5

Sex Crimes
From Renaissance to Enlightenment
W.M. NAPHY
'Wonderfully scandalous'
Diarmaid MacCulloch
£10.99
0 7524 2977 9

Ace of Spies The True Story of Sidney Reilly
ANDREW COOK
'The most definitive biography of the spying ace yet written… both a compelling narrative and a myth-shattering tour de force'
Simon Sebag Montefiore
£12.99
0 7524 2959 0

Tommy Goes To War
MALCOLM BROWN
'A remarkably vivid and frank account of the British soldier in the trenches'
Max Arthur
£12.99
0 7524 2980 4

If you are interested in purchasing other books published by Tempus, or in case you have difficulty finding any Tempus books in your local bookshop, you can also place orders directly through our website

www.tempus-publishing.com